I0160883

LITTLE BROTHERS

AND OTHER OBSERVATIONS

LITTLE BROTHERS
AND OTHER OBSERVATIONS

W. ROD OLSON

Halo
PUBLISHING
INTERNATIONAL

Copyright © 2025 W. Rod Olson. All rights reserved.

No part of this publication may be reproduced, stored in a retrieval system or transmitted in any form or by any means, electronic, mechanical, photocopying, recording or otherwise, without prior permission of Halo Publishing International.

The views and opinions expressed in this book are those of the author and do not necessarily reflect the official policy or position of Halo Publishing International. Any content provided by our authors are of their opinion and are not intended to malign any religion, ethnic group, club, organization, company, individual or anyone or anything.

No generative artificial intelligence (AI) was used in the writing of this work. The author expressly prohibits any entity from using this publication to train AI technologies to generate text, including, without limitation, technologies capable of generating works in the same style or genre as this publication.

For permission requests, write to the publisher, addressed "Attention: Permissions Coordinator," at the address below.

Halo
PUBLISHING
INTERNATIONAL

Halo Publishing International
7550 W IH-10 #800, PMB 2069,
San Antonio, TX 78229

First Edition, March 2025
ISBN: 978-1-63765-747-8
Library of Congress Control Number: 2025901013

The information contained within this book is strictly for informational purposes. Unless otherwise indicated, all the names, characters, businesses, places, events and incidents in this book are either the product of the author's imagination or used in a fictitious manner. Any resemblance to actual persons, living or dead, or actual events is purely coincidental.

Halo Publishing International is a self-publishing company that publishes adult fiction and non-fiction, children's literature, self-help, spiritual, and faith-based books. We continually strive to help authors reach their publishing goals and provide many different services that help them do so. We do not publish books that are deemed to be politically, religiously, or socially disrespectful, or books that are sexually provocative, including erotica. Halo reserves the right to refuse publication of any manuscript if it is deemed not to be in line with our principles. Do you have a book idea you would like us to consider publishing? Please visit www.halopublishing.com for more information.

To my cousin Marla,
whose
joie de vivre
since our shared childhoods in Edgemont
has continuously pushed me to be more,
to do more.

Contents

July 28, 1962

Grandma was sitting toward the left side of her red uphol-stered sofa, reading. She had only one lamp lit in the living room of her Marshall Heights home, the lamp that sat on the end table nearest the dining room. The lamp cast a dim shadow over the large, varnished, red-brick fireplace on the interior wall of the living room. Above the mantel, which was always crowded with framed photos of Grand-ma's grandchildren and wedding photos of her daughters, hung a large oil painting of a winter-forest scene opening onto a red barn. It was painted by Uncle Dale, the artist husband of Grandma's third daughter, Delores, whom we called Aunt Jinny.

I was across the room, sitting on a step, midway up the stairs to the second story of Grandma's home. The stairs had a landing about three steps above me; there the stairs turned to the right and continued ascending to the second floor. Grandma's upright piano sat below me, parallel to the stairs. At the base of the stairs was Grand-ma's huge, blue-damask-upholstered rocker, a rocker I loved to rock in.

Grandma had tried to put me to bed earlier, but six-year-old me wouldn't go. So after having dealt with ten of her own children, and now five grandchildren older than I, she let me be. I guess she knew sleep would eventually overcome my stubbornness and lead me down the stairs to cuddle next to her and fall into sleep.

Across from the fireplace was the front door, which opened to a large pillared porch that extended across the front of the house. Grandma's home was a symmetrical Craftsman-style home with the front door positioned in the middle of the front wall of the living room; the door was flanked by two sets of French doors. Anyone entering Grandma's living room through the front door seemed to make a dramatic entrance, whether intended or not, given the architecture of the house and the design of the living room.

That front door was suddenly flung open, and in walked my dad. As I was running down the stairs to meet him, he looked at me with a wide smile and said, "You have a little brother."

Grandma raised her head from her reading and smiled. I don't remember exactly what she said to her oldest son, whom she still called Billy, but I remember that it was something congratulatory while inquiring about my mom and the baby.

Dad was still smiling.

My young mind was processing what "little brother" really meant now that he seemed to be present in my life.

Grandma rose, walked over to Dad, and hugged her son, a son who had done quite well for himself by the age of thirty-nine and of whom she was very proud.

She had every right to be proud of her Billy. A veteran of the Army Medical Corps during WWII, he had just celebrated his eighth anniversary as postmaster of the then-bustling town of Black Lick; had served as the cochairman of the sesquicentennial celebration of the town; was an active member of the local volunteer fire company; had just overseen the design, construction, and dedication of the new post office in town; was in the process of building a new ranch-style home in the subdivision of Edgemont; and was married to a beautiful and industrious wife from a prominent local family, my mom. And now, he was the father of two sons, the first two boys to carry forward the Olson name into the next generation.

Without hesitation, I decided at that moment that I wanted to buy a gift for my newly acquired "little brother" and was still processing what that meant. I was insisting. It was a Saturday night around ten. Time in a child's mind is sometimes nebulous. Time in a stubborn child's mind means nothing.

When we departed Grandma's home, we delivered the news of my new little brother to Aunt Helen and Uncle Bob. They had recently moved into a house down the street from our Edgemont home, which was still under construction, after previously living in an apartment up the block from our former home on Walnut Street. Their new home was a green-shingled, two-story house that had been moved by the state of Pennsylvania from the "old town" of Black Lick during the Conemaugh Dam Project of 1936, which resulted in one-half of my childhood hometown of Black Lick becoming a runoff site for the dam, all to protect the city of Johnstown.

Aunt Helen greeted us at her front door with a smile. She, too, had a red sofa, and she had not yet replaced her green wall-to-wall carpeting with the sculpted red wall-to-wall carpeting that later became a signature look in her homes. Two-and-a-half-year-old Linda was asleep in bed by now, so the conversation was in hushed tones. Aunt Helen had been waiting for the news of the birth.

Dad told her the details and said that "Vish is doing well." My dad's family used the nickname Vish for Mom; my mom's family used the nickname Vease.

I chimed into the conversation when an opening occurred and, looking up at Aunt Helen, told her that I needed to buy a gift for my little brother.

I remember Dad saying to Aunt Helen, "Do you have something Rodney can give to his brother as a gift?"

Dad's youngest sister, Helen, collected porcelain dogs. She walked out of her living room, in which we were standing, and returned with two of her porcelain dogs. The smaller of the two was brown with white-fur trim around its neck. It was in a reclined position. The second porcelain dog was white with black markings and in a standing-pointer position on a blue-speckled base. The standing dog was designed to be a planter.

I was satisfied. The little dog was for my little brother; the larger dog on the blue base was my gift for Mom.

After departing Aunt Helen and Uncle Bob's home, we headed to Aunt Della and Uncle Mario's home in Edgemont. We had moved out of our two-story, yellow-clapboard home with the pillared front porch and brown shutters on Walnut Street (a.k.a. Church Street) and were temporarily living with Aunt Della, Uncle Mario, Nancy, and Marla. Construction on our new home in Edgemont was still ongoing and would not be completed until October, well after I started first grade.

To this day, I often wonder why we moved out of that house. It was a beautiful home with pocket doors on the main level, a formal dining room with a built-in china and linen cabinet and a grand staircase with a landing leading to the second floor. The second floor boasted a wide, curved hallway, which ended on one side with a black- and white-tiled bathroom and on the other with my bedroom. The home had a breakfast nook, a walk-in pantry, two porches, one of which was screened, and an unused room on the third level that was finished and had a dresser in it. I suspect it was once a room for a maid. All the rooms were quite large, including mine with its cowboy wallpaper and nursery rhymes, which Mom had framed and hung on the walls.

I remember my cousins Nancy and Marla and I could jump on the mattress on the bed in the spare bedroom on the second floor and not be heard. Well, most of the time.

While living with Aunt Della and Uncle Mario, our furniture was in storage in the white, two-story house to the left of our former home. That house was then owned by our family friend Angelo, who was eventually elected to the office of district magistrate. He and his family had not yet moved into it, and Angelo and his wife, Ruth, allowed Mom and Dad to store our furniture there until our new home was completed. I guess our yellow, two-story home sold more quickly than Mom and Dad expected. It was bought by Dr. Herbie's brother. Dr. Herbie was a childhood friend of Mom and Dad's, his mother was best friends with my other grandma, and now—and most important to July 28, 1962—he was the doctor who delivered my new "little brother."

I remember well the furniture going into storage, but don't remember the day of the actual move of it to our new home. I remember because my black-and-white, stuffed panda bear and plush dog ended up "packed."

The next time I saw them was during the unpacking. Both had gotten wet in the move and now, to my startled disappointment, were damp and had the stuffing coming out of them.

Some things from childhood we never forget.

Dad woke me early on Sunday morning, July 29. After having a breakfast of cereal with Marla, Dad and I headed out in the tan-and-white 1959 Mercury Montclair that he and Mom now owned. Dad had bought a box of cigars after leaving the hospital the night before and had them in the car. I remember the cigars had a white stork on their blue cigar bands, indicating "It's a boy!" We stopped at many homes that morning so Dad could give cigars to his friends as he announced with pride that Mom and he "had a boy!"

I was still wondering what "little brother" was all about as we went from house to house, front door to front door.

I distinctly remember going to our former home with its pillared front porch and brown shutters on Walnut Street. Dad parked the car in front of it. The street was nearly empty of cars for a Sunday morning. With both the Methodist and Presbyterian churches on the same block as our house, the street filled up with parked cars in the morning on Sundays during the Methodist and Presbyterian church services. To announce my little brother's birth, Dad must have had me out and about well before the church services.

We walked up the front sidewalk of our former home and onto the porch. I remember the strange feeling I had being on our porch, which was no longer ours. Dad knocked on our former door.

Dr. Herbie's brother came to the door, opened the door that was no longer our door, and looked at us through the screen door that was no longer our screen door. After Dad told him the news about my little brother, Dr. Herbie's brother smiled wide, opened the door to shake Dad's hand, and as he did, Dad offered him a cigar.

My mind, during all of this, was processing Dr. Herbie's brother opening the door of our former home and, for that matter, being in our former home. This was piled on top of the matter of my new "little brother."

***

When Mom and Dad brought Bobby home (my little brother now had a name) from the hospital to Aunt Della and Uncle Mario's home, there was a constant flow of relatives and family friends to see him.

All of Mom's family loved his thick black hair and agreed, "He's a little Italian."

Aunt Giggi always referred to him as "the *bambino*."

All of Dad's family said, "He's a little Bernini."

Aunt Della and Uncle Mario had not yet remodeled their kitchen, but Aunt Della always had a chair positioned to the right of the dining room window, a window adjacent to the kitchen. I remember that it was there that Mom would often sit, cloth diaper thrown over her left shoulder, and feed my new little brother his bottle.

Nancy and Aunt Della took turns with Mom. Nancy was fourteen years old and in her glory when she got to hold, walk, or feed my little brother. She really enjoyed giving him attention.

Well, for that matter, everyone did. My little brother was certainly the center of attention. As the now youngest of the second generation of Mom's large Italian family, he held a special place in the hearts of my aunts, uncles, and older cousins. As the second to carry the Olson name of Dad's equally large family, he held an equally special place in the hearts of Dad's family, too.

As for Marla and me, we learned a new and often-repeated directive from our parents:

"Shhhh. Be quiet. The baby's sleeping."

Marla and I were often found peering over the sides of the bassinet in which my new little brother slept. He was always sleeping, eyes closed, face framed by that full head of black baby hair, always wrapped tight in a blanket. Sometimes, though, his hands were exposed, his tiny, tiny baby fingers clenched in fists.

Marla and I spent many hours playing in Aunt Della and Uncle Mario's basement, where we thought we couldn't be heard, until a voice exclaimed in hushed tones from the top of the basement steps:

"Shhhh. Be quiet. The baby's sleeping."

My little brother suddenly appeared and was assimilated into my life. My mind back then seemed to only register the moments. I don't think my young mind ever really processed any of it. Everything "just was." Perhaps this is how young minds work. They just take everything in and store it for processing another day, in another year, sometime in the future.

The gaps between the intake and storage of that time are significant for me. They always were. Perhaps it was all too much for my young mind to register then—a new "little brother," a move from the only home I had ever known, living with Aunt Della and Uncle Mario, and now being reminded of the really big unknown directly in front of me, "starting first grade," whatever that meant.

Aunt Della and Uncle Mario's home used well water; our new home was to have "city water." To avoid Bobby changing waters so early in his life and risking tummy troubles for him, Mom asked her friend Irene if she could supply Mom with city water from her home for my little brother to start life with.

Irene's home was about a block away from Aunt Della and Uncle Mario's home. Aunt Della owned a green, two-quart thermos with a handle, so every day Marla and I left Aunt Della and Uncle Mario's home with that thermos, walked down the sloping sidewalk in front of their house, then turned right onto the sidewalk parallel to Blaire Road, walked past the stone wall, which Uncle Mario had built to support their elevated front yard, to the intersection of Catalpa Street, in front of the Keiths' home. We looked both ways then crossed Blaire Road on our way to Irene's home, which sat on Catalpa Street across from Burrell Elementary School. Along the way, we talked, swung the thermos (sometimes over our heads), and held hands partway.

This was a big deal for me, as it was the first time I was permitted to walk anywhere without Mom or Dad with me. I did have Marla, who was a year older than I, for my guidance and protection, but I have no doubt that Aunt Della was watching our progress with that green thermos from the picture window of her living room each day.

When we arrived, we simply opened the screen door of Irene's back porch and walked up two steps into Irene's kitchen. After Irene took the thermos, filled it up, secured the lid, and handed it back to me, we were on our way after some interaction with her kids, our friends Rita and Gene. There was no swinging the thermos on the way back to Marla's house; it was too heavy.

***

I still can see Aunt Della carrying infant Bobby up the landing steps into her kitchen on the day he was baptized. Mom and Dad chose Aunt Della and Uncle Mario as Bobby's godparents. Bobby was in an all-white Baptismal outfit with a white cap. Wisps of his black hair peeked out from under his white cap. His Baptismal blanket was wrapped around him, cascading down in front of Aunt Della as she cradled him in her arms. Uncle Mario was behind her, followed by Mom and Dad. Nancy babysat Marla and me while they were all at Saint Francis Church in Graceton for the Baptism.

Everyone looked so happy and so elegant that day. Bob was silent, perhaps sleeping after all the morning activity, as Mom and Dad, Aunt Della and Uncle Mario entered the house. Marla and I stood mesmerized in the kitchen; Nancy was behind us.

***

My little brother had an endearing quality as a youngster. Before guests left our home, he was quick to run up to them and in his young voice, say:

> *"Goodbye. Good night. Come back.*
> *I'll see you tomorrow!"*

That little guy went on to live in over 110 countries for significant amounts of time in his career. He was fortunate to have dinner with President Ronald Reagan and to meet President Reagan's wife, Nancy. On a flight out of Kathmandu, the pilot announced that Mount Everest was on the left side of the plane. Bob was eager to take in the view, but just then President Jimmy Carter stood up in his section and introduced himself to everyone. Bob often jokes that he couldn't decide which was more important, meeting President Carter or seeing Mount Everest.

I wish I could remember more about my little brother from that early time in our lives, but the memories are sequestered in my brain, comfortably tucked somewhere inside my subconscious. Perhaps someday, or in another time or life, they will emerge again, and, hopefully, these moments for me then will be interconnected streams of consciousness in full, living color.

They say the perception of time speeds up as you grow older. I have often felt this. I am not troubled by this, however, as by doing so, it brings the past closer to the present.

No Less than an A on That Report Card

My parents, like most parents, had a few sayings that continue to resonate with my brother and me. For Mom, they were:

Turn it into a prayer.

Family comes first.

*Don't talk about the family
outside of the family.*

That's none of your business. Stay out of it.

Did you finish your homework? Let me see it.

*If you're not going to do it right,
don't do it at all.*

*Stai zitto! (Shut up! Saved for
public locations.)*

And her two most memorable:

Some things are best left unsaid.

What the heck's the matter with you?

And for Dad:

> *No less than an A on that report card.*
>
> *You are not competing against*
> *anyone but yourself.*
>
> *What did you learn in school today?*
>
> *That is not dinner conversation.*
>
> *Money doesn't grow on trees.*
>
> *Here's twenty bucks. Spend it wisely.*
>
> And when older,
>
> *Did you visit your grandmother?*

Dad taught my brother and me "to always take the high road" and, to quote Ralph Waldo Emerson, "how to endure the betrayal of false friends."

By example and lesson, he taught us to be humble about accomplishments. He taught us to be gentlemen, to hold the door for Mom, to carry the groceries for her, and to always give her, Grandma and our godmothers both a hello and a goodbye kiss. He taught us, too, to never forget our small-town roots.

When I moved to New York City, I never thought about losing my small-town roots. But I never thought what "small-town roots" meant at that time in my life either. As years passed, a true understanding of this foundation started to become clear to me...and relevant. Now, it is important. I am grateful for my small-town roots and grateful for my parents' sayings, which continue to be part of my life.

Some of those sayings, no doubt, were meant to be disciplinary. Some of them were directional. I don't think my brother or I ever felt constrained by them; they were never delivered in a forceful or angry way. "Turn it into a prayer" often comes to mind now, during my daily life. "Family comes first" and "Don't talk about the family outside of the family" are ingrained in my DNA. Dad always meant it when, at the dinner table, my brother or I brought up a subject that elicited, "That is not dinner conversation," and he never handed back our report cards without a demanding "No less than an A on that report card." But both admonitions were more instructional and encouraging than chastisements.

Yes, Mom and Dad did discipline us as kids when it was necessary. Corner standing was among my punishments. Spending hours in our rooms was there too, although this wasn't so bad as I had a bookshelf full of *Hardy Boys* mysteries to read, and my brother had his bookshelf of the *World Book Encyclopedia*, which he could pour over for hours on end. Later in life, we both would have our driving privileges suspended. I don't think either of us was ever "grounded."

The efforts of daily life and raising two boys all would come to a halt in the evenings after dinner when homework was completed. Late spring, summer, and early autumn evenings were spent on the back porch on our porch swing, glider, and multiple lawn chairs, or sitting in the yard until the mosquitos started buzzing. Sometimes our next-door neighbors Elee and Joe and Mrs. Shields, the retired schoolteacher, whose home was on the other side of Elee and Joe's, joined us. Sometimes Betty, who lived on the other side of our home, came over, leaned on the brick half wall surrounding our porch, and talked. Often, Aunt Della, Uncle Mario, and Marla dropped in unexpectedly, or Aunt Nellie and Uncle Clarence did. Sometimes Dad's youngest sister, Helen, and her husband, my uncle Bob, pulled their car into our driveway and visited for a while.

If Mom had made a great dessert, it was shared. If she had a leftover from dinner that Uncle Mario enjoyed, he had a plate of it served to him. While all of this was going on, Marla and I played in the yard, but mostly we just sat, spoke when spoken to, and took in the adults' conversations. If something wasn't for our ears, Mom, Aunt Della, and Aunt Nellie switched to Italian. Marla, my brother, and I just accepted the fact that we were to be excluded when Italian was spoken; the conversation wasn't meant for our ears. If gardens needed to be watered or when the fireflies started to appear, conversations ended, and our guests left. And often, too, we reciprocated by visiting them when Mom said to Dad, "Hey, Bill, let's go up to Della and Mario's," or "Let's take a drive to Homer City to see my sister Nellie."

I read a book review in the newspaper, *La Nostra Voce*, the monthly newspaper published by the Italian Sons and Daughters of America. I was intrigued and quick to order the book. The book is entitled, *Secrets of Italian Self Care*, written by Dr. Eugene Antenucci. In it, Dr. Antenucci speaks of *"dolce far niente,"* the sweetness of doing nothing. For a person from the United States, surrounded by up-to-the-minute communications through technology and constant bombardment by the news and social media, this concept was certainly intriguing. For the New Yorker I have evolved into, it was inconceivable.

But in thinking back over my childhood and the evenings on the back porch or on lawn chairs in our yard or the yard of family and friends, unbeknownst to me at the time, this is what I experienced: dolce far niente. I am sure this downtime, this quiet time shared with others, was passed down from previous generations. Other than watching the eleven-o'clock news before going to bed, there was no one glued to the television, no cell phones, no internet. Games that were played by us kids were physical and played in the yards or on boards at the kitchen table. If the telephone in the kitchen rang, Mom or Dad leisurely rose from their chairs to answer it. If they missed the call, no issue. Later, when an answering machine was introduced into our home, sometimes the telephone ringing would result in, "Let the answering machine pick it up. I'll call them back later."

Relaxed, yes.

Focused on relaxing, yes.

The family and friends present and around us more important than those transmitted electronically via telephone line, yes.

We kids sitting with the adults, learning while listening to life stories, yes.

All this in my life today, no.

I can't speak for the rest of the United States, but my life as a New Yorker does not echo this lifestyle, a lifestyle I associate with my small-town roots, but also a lifestyle I associate with a time that is in my past. But it is not for me a time that has "passed." I find myself often thinking about how to go back to this style of living, stopping for the evening and enjoying quiet conversation with family and friends in a relaxed setting. I am afraid I will not find it in high-rise living in New York City. Since moving here, I have known my neighbors through random conversations in hallways. This is usual for New York high-rise living. Getting together with friends aren't "drop-in" moments. Visits to relax with friends are scheduled and usually involve going somewhere for dinner in the din of a restaurant with meaningful waitstaff intermittently interrupting to see if you need anything.

I often tell people I want to move to a cabin on a lake in the woods. The cabin needs to be within walking distance of a fresh, in-season produce stand; a market that sells fresh meat, fish, and cheese; and a wine store. I will also need dairy, as I hope to buy milk, butter, and yogurt from a local dairy farm, as my family did when I was a kid. My only technology will be electricity and on the wall of my kitchen a beige rotary phone with a twenty-foot cord that reaches to a front porch that faces the lake.

My business partner, Kim, shares some of the same dreams and wants her cabin in the same woods, across the lake from me. No cell phone. She wants a rowboat to row across the lake when she wants to talk with me—just a rowboat for our communications. Kim at one time had her cell phone programmed with the cannon stanza from the *1812 Overture* for my ringtone. Need I say more?

The beige phone is a throwback to the beige rotary phone that sat on the kitchen counter of our new ranch-style home when I was a kid. Today, that counter would be called a peninsula; back then it was just called a "counter with barstools on one side," the kitchen on the other. After putting my little brother to bed for his afternoon nap, Mom could often be found on one of the barstools at this counter, talking to one of her sisters, Grandma Olson, or one of her friends on that beige rotary phone.

Sometimes Elee would walk into the kitchen, and the telephone conversation would end as Mom moved to make coffee and settle down at the kitchen table to talk with Elee over coffee. Elee drank from a mug; when Mrs. Shields dropped in, Mom always served coffee in a cup and saucer. But there was never any hurry for them. They enjoyed conversation over a leisurely cup of coffee in the middle of the afternoon.

I often sat there listening until my friend Joey would show up at the back door or Mom suggested I "go outside and play." Once while sitting at the table, listening to the Fuller Brush man present his brushes to Mom (he had just come from Elee's home), a stray pair of scissors on the kitchen table found their way into my young hands. The Fuller Brush man packed up his brushes suddenly and departed as Mom loudly exclaimed something after I cut a large swathe of hair from my head, all the way down to my scalp.

Those afternoons when I was home from school and with my mom and her friends, or in the evenings when Cousin Marla and I sat contentedly listening to the adults on our back porch, were serving as another learning experience for our young selves. Subconsciously, they were teaching a lesson that I now have come to fully appreciate, a lesson that cannot be learned in a book, but is taught only by experiencing it. And as I look back on those times, dolce far niente is what I was learning. And what Marla and my little brother were learning. I don't know if Mom and Dad were aware of the lesson they were giving us then. This lesson was not as overt as their oft-said phrases. But it was a lesson nonetheless.

As conversations during those evenings progressed, family was often the topic. But family was always discussed in a supportive manner. I never once heard my mom or her brothers and sisters talk negatively about one of their siblings. Family situations were discussed, but the conversations were always of a supportive nature.

If a neighbor approached our porch, all discussions of family suddenly ceased, as if they had never occurred. I remember this. Mom often said to my brother and me, "Family comes first," and we witnessed her and her siblings living her saying. This saying had to have been handed down from her parents to Mom and her seven siblings. This phrase certainly remained as cemented in our minds through words and observations as those lessons we learned in school, the ones my brother and I were to turn into As on our report cards.

Years ago, when I was in Rome, Rein, the former husband of a friend from the Netherlands, said to me over dinner one evening, "*Piano*." It was a lovely evening of outdoor dining in a piazza filled with other diners, all slowly enjoying the evening, the scenery, the wine, and their meals of various Italian delicacies served family style by an impeccable professional waitstaff under a clear, starry Italian sky. The day had been a busy one, and I guess I was showing it in my manner and in my conversation. Rein said it again to me, but this time he gestured a downward motion with his hands as he said it. I then got the meaning of his Italian and his hand motion: slow down. Not just "slow down," but "Slow yourself down and into the moment." Rein brought me back for a moment to a time on our back porch when I was a kid, sitting there with my parents. Rein's phrase and gesture are still with me.

Would I have fully understood Rein's statement had I not been that kid on the back porch with my parents? I'm not sure. Did Mom and Dad ever think that memories of those evenings on the back porch would find their way into my mind during an evening in Rome? I'm not sure either. But, thanks to Mom and Dad, I have an appreciation of those evenings, those moments, those times of dolce far niente.

I now find myself working hard to relearn this form of relaxation and incorporate it into a very different non-stop lifestyle into which I once was excitedly drawn as a resident of New York City. And with this effort to relearn, I once again hear my dad saying:

> *"You are not competing against anyone but yourself."*

Saint Valery-en-Caux

I have been thinking a lot lately about my dad's time in the Army Medical Corps in France during World War II. My brother and I knew that Grandma Olson had not heard from Dad in a while, and a buddy of his wrote to Grandma to inform her that he was okay. We also knew that Dad was in a train wreck in France during his time in World War II. But the details of this, if Dad ever told us, were forgotten. But, I seriously doubt that Dad spoke of the train wreck, as he never talked about his time in World War II.

In recent research on the train wreck, my brother uncovered several articles dictated by soldiers, later in life, who had been in the same wreck, experiencing the same things as Dad. I did have, in a scrapbook, several articles mentioning the train wreck, but no details about it. Those articles accompanied the letter to Grandma, the one informing her that Dad was okay. By then, they were yellowed and fragile with age. But the articles my brother uncovered explained the train wreck in detail…wrenching detail. Suddenly Dad's decision not to speak about his time in the army made sense. His experiences were to be consciously relegated to his subconscious. They were not subject matter to be discussed with his sons, certainly not when we were young, or even later when we were older.

By late December 1944, the initial success of Adolf Hitler's Ardennes offensive spurred the Americans to ship all available reinforcements to the European Theater of Operations (ETO). Army units of all descriptions hastened to complete their training in the United States and were ordered to Europe instead of their original destinations in the Pacific. The first convoy to proceed directly to France from the United States cast off from New York on January 1, 1945.

Dad was in this first convoy, one of eighty-five men in the 553rd Ambulance Company. Arriving in Le Havre, France, after witnessing the ship next to theirs hit a mine, Dad's company marched two miles in winter's frigid temperatures to Camp Lucky Strike, a staging camp with room for 66,000 military personnel. Together with 580 tons of soldiers and army equipment, Dad boarded a forty-five-unit 40–8 boxcar train headed to Saint Valery-en-Caux on the coast of Normandy. The boxcars were named 40–8s because they could hold either forty men or eight horses. The boxcars had no heat. The troops slept on the wooden floors of the drafty boxcars. They were in them during winter's cold for nine hours; the trip was only scheduled to take four.

In an effort to speed troops to the front, it was later reported that the train departed the station despite knowing that it had faulty brakes. At the top of a hill leading into Saint Valery-en-Caux, the brakes began to fail. The subsequent crash accordioned most of its cars. The first ten boxcars were piled on top of each other as high as the roof of the Saint Valery-en-Caux train station; those boxcars behind pyramided even higher. Dad's company was in the first four boxcars. His car was among the top cars piled up at the station; it had actually crashed into the train station itself. The engine flew through the back of the station.

Dad was standing in the open doorway of his boxcar and was thrown free of the crash, sustaining only a sprained ankle. His best friend, Robert E. Mowry, was eating K rations in the back of the same boxcar when the crash occurred. He had his leg broken above the knee and had to be airlifted to a hospital in Chicago. Of their company of eighty-five, thirty-three were killed, and twenty-eight were injured, leaving twenty-four alive without significant injuries. Dad was alive and among the uninjured, save for his sprained ankle.

To read about the crash scene is gut-wrenching. It is a story that, with all due respect to those who experienced it, shall remain with their memories and not discussed here. And with respect to Dad, it will remain with him, in his deepest memories, where he wanted this to remain.

Villagers were seen blessing themselves as they watched the train lose control as it approached their town at sixty miles per hour. In total, eighty-nine soldiers were killed, and 152 were reported injured. The scene was described as "chilling, bloody human carnage."

Dad, being one of the fortunate soldiers and part of the medical corps, had to go into action to tend to the injured and the dying. I can't begin to imagine what he witnessed and what he had to manage. And as soon as they could move forward, Dad and the remaining soldiers who were uninjured were pushed on into battle.

Both my brother and I were stunned and speechless when reading the articles his research produced. If we had been standing next to each other, I am sure we would have hugged. And I am sure it brought tears to my brother's eyes, as it did mine. The articles closed the gaps in the yellowed, fragile articles that accompanied Robert E. Mowry's letter to Grandma. But the knowledge itself has spurred my brother and me to continue research on this subject, not for publication, but to better understand the experience our Dad lived through on January 17, 1945. He was a hero for helping his injured train mates on that day.

To us, as our dad, he was always a hero, but now the definition of "hero" as it applies to Dad is much, much different for us. Much, much more. It is soul touching.

***

I am writing this soon after Halloween, 2023. My apartment building in New York City has a community room, indoor pool, simulated golfing room, laundry room, and outdoor terrace on the fourth floor. It also has a gym on that floor. When the elevator doors open to the fourth floor, they open to the sign-in desk for the gym. The people who manage the desk are friendly, often smiling at those of us staring blankly at them from the elevators when the doors open. They decorate the desk area and entrance to the gym for each holiday.

This Halloween, among the usual ghoul, fake spiderwebs, etc. was a plastic severed arm covered in painted blood. I guess somebody designed this, and somebody else put it on the market, and, now, somebody affiliated with the gym found it appropriate for a Halloween decoration. It turned my stomach every time I was forced to view it when the elevator doors opened. I avoided the scene as much as possible, though, during the month of October.

Have we as a society become so desensitized to tragedy and human suffering that people now find a severed, bloody plastic arm to be an appropriate decoration, Halloween or not?

Each time I saw this so-called decoration, I thought of what my dad experienced in real life at Saint Valery-en-Caux and after, during the battles of World War II, in his designated, dutiful service to support the injured and the dead.

Yes, I now fully understand why Dad never talked about his time in World War II.

And yes, it scares me to think, as a society, we may have become so desensitized to human suffering that we find a severed, bloody plastic arm an appropriate decoration.

***

The town of Saint Valery-en-Caux was liberated from Nazi rule by British forces on September 11, 1944. Fifty years later, on this same day, the residents of Saint Valery-en-Caux gathered at the rebuilt train station and dedicated a plaque that reads:

> *To the memory of the American soldiers come to free the soil of France who were killed accidentally at St. Valery-en-Caux. The 17th of January, 1945.*

Seeing this plaque in person is on my "must do" list for future travel, as I know it is for my brother.

It is important for us to be there together, to stand together and pay our respects for all this plaque represents for those who gave their lives. And for Dad.

Disco

I am back in Mexico City with my client here. The work started again last September when the CEO called me to relaunch a major project that was halted due to the pandemic. I am glad to be back, and it feels as if no time has passed, although it has. What we passed through during my last time here was a historic, worldwide, devastating pandemic.

I am no longer able to enjoy the serenity of the thirty-ninth-floor lounge of the Intercontinental Hotel while watching the stately volcano Popocatépetl emit puffs of steam and ash as I have my breakfast. I now go to Café Urbano, the restaurant on the mezzanine of the Intercontinental.

Café Urbano is a bit chaotic most days. The restaurant has achieved the feat of maximizing the greatest number of tables and people in the least amount of space, while adhering to capacity laws here in Mexico City. Not being a morning person, my trek through the hotel corridor each morning to a bank of elevators that takes me to a landing and a set of stairs that lead down to Café Urbano is rote activity for me. With my briefcase on wheels in tow, coupled with a Land's End black tote filled with files, the trip is a challenge each morning in my fog of half wakefulness.

The jolt of people and loud conversations in Café Urbano upon my arrival do little to add to my state of alertness.

But I must say that Café Urbano is a wonderful place for breakfast. The buffet is incredibly large, with the largest selection of breakfast options I have ever seen at a hotel breakfast buffet. The staff is overly attentive, and the customers are generally a lively mix of voices speaking French, forms of Asian, Italian, Spanish, and other languages. I find myself attentive to the Italian and French languages being spoken. Both remind me of missed opportunities in my life to learn these languages in my youth.

Especially troublesome for me is hearing Italian. The spoken language takes me back to my mom often saying when I was a wee one, "Come here, little one. I want to teach you Italian." I would have nothing to do with it. The memory is still very active in my mind, relegated to that area in our brains where the "You will regret this" file resides—a file that often pops open for me, flooding my thoughts with what could have been.

This past week, Café Urbano prepared fifteen breakfast boxes for me to take to Legaria for the technical team with whom I was working on a project. The boxes of two pastries, fresh-cut fruit (including figs!), and cups of yogurt were well received. This past week, too, I entered Café Urbano one day to the blaring sounds of "Disco Inferno." I took my seat after selecting a croissant and two cups of yogurt. My black coffee was already waiting for me. Head down with my breakfast and my cell phone—and once again seeming to block out all noise and distractions around me as I ate and frantically scrolled through texts, emails, and headlines on my phone—I suddenly realized my right foot was tapping to the beat of "Disco Inferno."

My brain had alerted a "feel good" memory file and sent a signal racing to my right foot to start tapping, and tapping, too, to the beat of the music. The signal bypassed my consciousness on the way down my spinal cord and into my foot. *No time for consciousness...we got to get that foot tapping. Now!*

I paused and looked up when my consciousness realized what my foot was doing.

I am convinced that there are few who won't find their foot tapping upon hearing "Disco Inferno." Whether you like disco or claim not to like disco, I believe everyone is moved in some way by the upbeat sounds of this genre of music. But "Disco Inferno" is the pinnacle in disco music. It doesn't get better.

I first came to listen to the sounds of disco as a junior at Saint Vincent College, but it always took second place to the Doobie Brothers, ELO, and the Eagles. During my senior year, I met Terry, a sophomore biology major, like me, from our sister college, Seton Hill. The two schools complemented each other in courses, and credits were gained in full when taking classes at either one, whether you were a guy at the all-male school of Saint Vincent or a gal at the all-female school of Seton Hill. The schools ran buses on the hour between their locations in Latrobe and Greensburg, Pennsylvania, a ride of about twenty minutes on a good-weather day.

I don't remember when or how I met Terry. She was a pretty young lady, about an inch taller than I, graceful in her movements and manners, slender, with black hair and delicate features, and, like me, wholly dedicated to her studies. I learned she had studied dance prior to being accepted into Seton Hill. During one of our conversations, the subject of disco came up, and we mutually agreed that she would teach me to disco dance. I was game. So we agreed that since Thursdays held few classes for either of us, Wednesday evenings would be good for her to come to my dorm room and teach me to dance. I think, too, that some of this stemmed from her looking for a dance partner, and I was willing, but this is my own speculation.

So, for months, Terry came to my room on Wednesdays, and as was customary for us Bearcats when girls were visiting, my roommate, Bill, would vacate the room so Terry could teach me to dance. As Bill was leaving to go to the library, there was often a wink and a "yeah…dancing" from him.

Terry always arrived with her disco album; I do not remember any longer the group it featured. But we would chat for a while, talk about classes, and then I would put the album on Bill's stereo, and we would begin. I must admit I was somewhat awkward in the beginning. Perhaps a challenge.

***

My mom wanted me to learn to dance around the same time I refused to learn Italian. The ability to dance ran in her family. All her sisters and brothers were adept at dance. My older cousins Betty Lou and Marlene took classes at the Wagner Dance Studio in Blairsville. Both were exceptional students. Marlene went on to win many contests for her agile abilities at dance, in which she incorporated her nimbleness in acrobatics. Mrs. Dunmire, a seamstress who lived up the block from us when we were still living in the two-story home on Walnut Street in Black Lick, designed and sewed Marlene's dance costumes. Marlene once told me that Mrs. Dunmire would sew, by hand, each sequin onto her outfits.

Mom knew Jimmy Wagner from taking Marlene to his dance classes. So she decided I would learn to dance.

Mom and Dad were known for their ability to jitterbug when they were young. When I attended my cousin Judy's wedding with them, I first saw them in action on the dance floor. Dad whipped Mom around, and Mom followed Dad's lead. Their bodies moved to the rhythm of the music while matching each other's rhythm. I can still see it.

At that same wedding, I watched my dad dance with my mom's sister, my aunt Giggi. Their moves were smooth and flawless. I think they were doing the rumba or something similar. I was too young to know what "rumba" was at that time.

Aunt Giggi and her husband, my uncle Miller, owned the Bernini Hotel in Black Lick during its glory days. In addition to the hotel itself—the rooms of which, when vacant, Aunt Giggi permitted me to explore as a kid—the hotel had a large reception hall where weddings and events were held. On Saturday nights, Mom often told me that when Aunt Giggi and Uncle Miller did not have events scheduled, they opened up the reception hall to the public for dancing to the sounds of the music of the 1940s and early 1950s. The room's adjacent bar retained its 1930s look of a glass-block bar, dark wood, banquet tables, and behind the bar, a large mirror in front of which sat stepped rows of liquor bottles. The glass block had pink and white neon shining through it. I remember because Aunt Giggi would often lift me onto a barstool and make a Shirley Temple for me. I must admit that I found more interest, though, in unwrapping the plastic swizzle stick that came with the drink, than the drink itself.

Mom and Dad; Aunt Della and Uncle Mario; Aunt Nellie and Uncle Clarence; Uncle Reno and Aunt Marian; Cousin Betty Lou and her husband, Raymo; and of course, Aunt Giggi and Uncle Miller would often spend Saturday evenings dancing and socializing as a family at the Bernini Hotel. Uncle Reno and Aunt Marian were amazing in their ability to waltz. These are memories some of my older cousins now cherish. As for my brother and me, we were still twinkles in the eyes of our parents then.

So after much discussion with me about learning to dance, the day came when Mom dressed me and got me ready to drive to Wagner's in our two-tone green Pontiac Chieftain. We were in the vestibule of our home. As Mom was putting my grey-tweed coat with matching cap on me, I froze then had a meltdown, crying that I wasn't going to Wagner's. Period. After much consoling and prodding by my mother, and my nonstop crying, Mom gave up. She must have been terribly disappointed. Well, I am sure she was terribly disappointed. That moment entered—no, stamped itself into—the area of my brain where the "You will regret this" file resides. And I do.

I wish I could say that I was too young to know what I was doing, but, honestly, in hindsight, I think I did know what I was doing. The scene all repeated itself when Mom wanted me to learn to play the piano. And this memory, also a regret, took residence next to the dance-memory regret. When surfacing in my memory, they do so together. I wonder when this area of our brains first starts to engage with our consciousness. It must be early in life. I was about four or five years old when it all happened. My brother had not been born yet.

I think the "You will regret this" area of our brains may have an unlimited capacity. But I also believe that, later in life, an area next to it starts to develop that counters the "You will regret this" with "Do it! You don't want to regret this." Maybe this area of our brains also says, "Look next door at that stash of regrets! Do you want to add another?!?!"

I now also like to think that what develops between these two areas is yet another area called "reason." It works hard later in life to manage the negotiations. I wish it had been there when I was once adamant about not learning Italian or taking dancing and piano lessons.

So perhaps we get wiser. Or reason becomes more dominant, sifting through the options of "to do" or "not to do."

Or perhaps, as we grow older, we listen more attentively to our guardian angels who provide direction and advice.

***

Terry and I practiced and practiced and practiced our dancing. Her graceful and deliberate movements countered my awkwardness and fear of embarrassment. It all started with a routine, then moved on to my giving her signals with my hands, on her back, of which way or how to move. And, even later, we practiced more difficult moves, such as my dipping her. Yep, you can imagine how that all went in the beginning. But we did get better, and eventually I asked Terry to a cotillion, which was being hosted by my senior class at Saint Vincent, where we danced in public. I smile as I think back on it.

One evening, Terry and I took the long drive from college back to my high school to see my brother in a concert. It was the first time my parents met her. They were very gracious, as I knew they would be. Dad made small talk while I could see Mom sizing her up and down. It was well known that Mom felt that no girl was good enough for her sons. And maybe even worse, Terry wasn't Italian.

Terry and I eventually went our separate ways after I graduated. I heard she is now a doctor of medicine. Our studies back then came before anything else, but I think we both enjoyed the dance practices and our close friendship. Sometimes we did study together when I could help her with the science courses I had already completed. Terry, too, had a calmness about her demeanor that often lowered the temperature of my anxieties about a class or an upcoming exam.

At the graduation party my mom and dad held for me, my cousin Nancy asked me to teach her to disco. I had seen her on the dance floor in the past. As a kid, she taught me how to do the twist, the swim, and the monkey, and how to cha-cha. Like her parents, she was a very good dancer, but apparently, due to being eight years older than I, she was not a contemporary of the disco era. We went into my parents' living room, and I put an album on their stereo. But it wasn't like dancing with Terry. For all I remembered, I could not transfer that knowledge from my brain to my hands and feet with Nancy. So after a while and a lot of cousinly laughs, we stopped.

***

I thought of Terry as "Disco Inferno" swirled around all of us in Café Urbano that morning. With my foot tapping, my brain sent a signal to my mouth to smile, once again bypassing my consciousness.

Perfection

I first saw Sally present at a shareholders' meeting I attended years ago in Ohio. She was the president of a retail division. The auditorium was large, filled to capacity, and ominously dark. I was fortunate to secure a seat toward the back of the auditorium, but within view of the spotlighted stage. My mind wandered as I sat listening to the speeches drone on.

When it was Sally's turn to present, she took center stage after entering with the deliberate walk of a professional model, while glancing sideways to her audience. Her speech was in hand. Her presence immediately caught my eye and snapped me out of my blank gaze into undefined space. When Sally began her speech, I recognized that she was unlike the other speakers. She had command of her voice, command of her prepared words, and, looking directly at her audience, had command of them.

I was enraptured. I listened intently as she spoke of the successes of her business and the growth under her leadership. She spoke openly about the issues the business faced, the decisions that were not successful, the opportunities of the coming year. Nothing was sugarcoated. She was straight on with the good and the not so good, the highs and the lows. Her voice was easy, steady, and at peace with the words that emerged. She spoke with continual enthusiasm, pausing at times to allow comments to register with her audience. She smiled as she looked around the room, engaging her audience, pulling them in. And she said thank you at her conclusion.

I was about ten years into my retail career at that time. To date in my career, I had never heard a speaker like her. I wanted to work for her.

Soon after the shareholders' meeting, the retail-trade papers announced that Sally had accepted the position as president of a prominent women's specialty-store retailer headquartered on Fifty-Seventh Street in New York City. I raced to update my resume to hand deliver it to Sally's new executive assistant in New York. The next day, I received call a from her assistant, asking if I could meet Sally in her private conference room the next morning.

Could?!?!? WOW! My answer was a calm and professional "Why, of course. What time should I be there?" which was a complete disconnect from the excitement of my heart pounding in my chest and my mind flooding with gratefulness.

The next day, I was suited with my necktie tied in the perfect Windsor knot as Sally's assistant ushered me into her conference room. The next moment, the adjoining door to her office opened and Sally entered. She was smiling as she extended her hand. We sat at her conference table for about an hour. It wasn't the usual interview. I was not asked to explain my career up to that point, nor did I need to answer questions about my strengths and weaknesses or my greatest career accomplishment to date or what kind of tree would I be. Sally went straight to questions about my knowledge of retail and my understanding of the intricacy and nuances of the ever-moving, ever-evolving, mercurial area of retail called merchandise planning. Yes, straight to my knowledge. I don't think she ever looked down at my resume sitting in front of her. I liked our discussion. I liked her. She smiled a lot. What was happening was more of a conversation than an interview. I didn't need to prove myself.

At the end of our hour together, she told me she was leaving for Europe the next day. I was ready for the "we'll be in touch" ending of many interviews. But Sally looked me in the eyes and at that moment, while smiling, asked me if I would accept the job she was offering.

I loved working for Sally. She was hired to turn a business around, inject new energies, bring the product up-to-date, and expand the customer base. Every day was a new level of challenge. We all worked hard. I often found myself leaving the office at ten at night, stopping at Rue 57, the corner French restaurant one block from our offices, for a burger and glass of red wine, then walking home thirty blocks to release energy, only to do it all again the next day. I loved it. And yes, I would have burgers at a French restaurant.

I had to implement new processes with my existing staff, while keeping them engaged with the ever-evolving work and longer hours, and push them to their personal best. Suddenly, many of them were being called on in

meetings by Sally to report on their businesses. I nurtured
their comfort with presenting the knowledge they owned.
New presidents and consultants always bring the fear of
people losing their jobs, and I knew I was dealing with
those fears among my team.

Evolve and grow we did. I was in my element. After
a year, our growth was outpacing the ability of my team to
keep up with it. While on a trip with Sally and our senior
team to the West Coast to visit stores, Sally took me aside
as we walked through an open-air mall. She put her hand
on my shoulder, looked at me, and asked me how I was
doing. She then asked me if I needed anything.

I answered, "Yes, I need more analysts to keep up with
our growth." When she asked me how many positions
I needed to add, I knew the answer already. "Ten," I said.
She said she would ask Gerri, head of human resources,
to conduct a job fair for me so we could fill the positions.
In two months, they were all filled, many analysts coming
from Wall Street firms.

Working with Sally, I grew to understand the driving
force within her and her required expectations for her
direct reports: strive for perfection. It was just that simple.
As long as we were demonstrating that we were striving
for perfection in our work, she was pleased and supportive. For me, I had reached career Xanadu.

Sally established two benchmarks for me in my retail
career: One for my expectations of excellence in my supe-
riors. The other was the same expectation for myself and

my direct reports. She set an example for me that I have worked to emulate since then.

I love the story my friend Andrea shared with me when Sally interviewed her for her role as head of stores. Andrea visited a few stores beforehand. She took a white glove with her and in one store swiped the shelf displaying shoes. The glove was grey with dust. Andrea presented the glove to Sally during their interview conversation. Andrea got the job.

***

Irving Thalberg was known as the Boy Wonder of MGM, the mastermind behind its explosive growth and success in the early years. I have read and studied a lot about him and his career. I often have called him my mentor, although he passed in 1936, a generation or two before my time. He left behind an expansive legacy of how to build and run a movie studio, together with a vast treasure of notable and Oscar-winning movies. Chance led Irving to a meeting with Louis B. Mayer, then a small movie-studio owner in California. After Mayer's merger with two other movie studios to become Metro-Goldwyn-Mayer, Irving, at the age of twenty-six, was appointed head of production for MGM by Mr. Mayer. Irving's genius drove MGM to become the most prominent movie studio of the 1930s and 1940s. Irving's drive for perfection sealed MGM's reputation for quality movies, movies whose reputation still exists today.

Irving's biographies were page-turners for me. I read one of them several times over the years and have it handy on my bookshelf to return to when I feel the need for inspiration. He left behind a treasure trove of quotes, many of which hold special places in my quote collection. Among them:

Never let your standards be less than great.

Credit you give to yourself
isn't worth having.

Nobody can teach you anything from his own
experience, but he can find a key to you
and make you open yourself up to reach the
highest power you can reach, to make you
never stop thinking.

For a young man, Irving developed a management style that once I had read about it, became another of my guiding forces. He surrounded himself with managers who complemented his own talents. He knew his knowledge limitations, and he supplemented them with experts he could trust and, to some extent, befriend. He socialized regularly with his managers. All this was done in Irving's quest for perfection.

Sadly, Irving passed at the young age of thirty-seven from a congenital heart disease. Having produced over 400 movies during his MGM career, some of which are still the greatest ever made, and having found and nurtured some of the biggest stars in the history of the movie industry, he never permitted his name to be placed on any of his movies during his lifetime.

***

If you read biographies of Irving Thalberg, you will find he had significant challenges in his career. Certainly, every day was not a cakewalk for Sally and our team either. Challenges sometimes were easy, sometimes great, sometimes lasting for a few days, sometimes for weeks. But Sally and Irving charged right into the middle of them like knights on white horses. I remember the conversations with Sally, sometimes one-on-one, about paths to solutions. During one of these moments, Sally said to me:

You can't move a mountain all at once,

but you can move it one tablespoon at a time.

It is a quote that remains with me and sits proudly among my collection of quotes.

Our offices were in the same building as those of Diana Ross. Once, Sally and I entered an elevator, only to find ourselves standing next to Ms. Ross. A beautiful woman, Ms. Ross was poised and dignified in her stance. She looked at us and gave us that familiar elevator nod of recognition accompanied by a slight smile. Personally, I did not know where to look, but I wanted to keep my gaze on Ms. Ross during that once-in-a-lifetime moment. Sally gave me her wide, knowing smile and continued her pre-elevator conversation with me. It was a lesson that registered in my memory bank of professional conduct.

And I remember once, in a meeting with our senior staff, one of the members started to say, "I feel..." Sally was quick to say, "Thank you, but this is not about feelings. This is about business decisions." Straight and to the point. She was right. I have never, since then, used the word "feelings" or any of its derivations in a business conversation.

But Sally was always right there on the front lines with us. She once explained to our team that you can make as much money or more by keeping prices "customer-friendly" and selling more, than by raising prices to increase profits. She not only explained this, she had us test it to prove to her team that this was possible. I know. I was part of the executive decision and reported the results. She didn't hand out directives; she was right there with us, in the middle of the initiatives.

Over my career, I have noticed a quality in the leaders I consider great. They tend to share the same foundation, the same core DNA. I have had the great fortune of working later in my career with others, but Sally was the first of this caliber. Clearly, she left an impression on me and a mark on my career. So did Irving Thalberg. So did my dad.

***

During my early life, the leadership qualities my dad possessed never registered with me. He was who he always was, my dad. Yes, my dad gave speeches. Yes, my dad belonged to and led sometimes too many organizations. Yes, my dad drove himself to rise to prominence in the

US Postal Service in the state of Pennsylvania. Yes, my dad made my brother and me attend some conventions with him and my mom. Yes, my dad ushered my brother and me to the sacristy of Saint Bonaventure Church after Mass one Sunday morning and told our priest, Father Kowal, that he wanted us to be altar boys. And when I hit my teenage years, yes, my dad suggested that I become a lector in that same church. Yes, my dad taught me to have a very firm handshake and look the recipient in the eyes at the same time.

And yes, my dad would always say, "Nothing less than an A on that report card." But it was never with pressure. This came with an oft-repeated phrase from both Mom and Dad: "You are not competing against anyone but yourself." My brother and I took these phrases to heart. They are quotes I now repeat, giving credit where credit is due: to Mom and Dad. I now understand it was my parents' way of guiding their sons to strive for internal personal perfection.

During my formative years I never did realize the impact my dad was having on my life and the direction he was giving me. Growing up, one day he was sitting on the living room floor with me, putting an HO train set together under our Christmas tree; another day he presented me with a uniform that matched his, the one he wore when he played for our town's softball league. When I hit fourth grade, we sat at our kitchen table as he taught me how to make book covers from brown paper bags, in the same way he did as a kid sitting at Grandma Olson's kitchen table. He instructed me to write the names of each subject on the book covers, but do so before putting the covers on the books so my new purple marker would not bleed onto the actual jacket of the book.

I must admit that it was a somewhat nervous moment for my brother and me when we started our altar-boy duties. Until Mrs. Colesar measured us for our personal cassocks, which she made, we were given cassocks once worn by older, "now-retired" altar boys. Mrs. Colesar made all the cassocks for us altar boys then. She also made my mom's wedding gown, veil, and train years prior. I was equally nervous my first Sunday serving as lector. But I had my dad to emulate that Sunday, as he too was a lector, and I had unconsciously watched him in his duties for many years. Dad had me practice the readings beforehand and gave me pointers to engage the congregation; to this day as a lector, I still practice the readings before my turns as lector on Sundays. And I am conscious to speak with Dad's slow and deliberate manner, putting emphasis where needed.

Our grades in school were important to my parents, and they became equally important to my brother and me. I didn't know until high school, when I spent time perusing my parents' yearbooks, that they both graduated cum laude. I was perusing yearbooks; my brother was reading the *World Book Encyclopedia* for fun. When an opportunity for extra credit arose in class, I always jumped on it with my parents' support. I remember doing a report on Caesar Rodney, a signer of the Declaration of Independence from Delaware (funny, I still remember the state he represented). I chose him at the suggestion of Joe Hamilton, a former teacher who was now the clerk in my dad's post office, but also for the obvious reason of our shared name. I remember writing my report on Caesar Rodney in slow, steady cursive on white, lined composition paper. After I finished handwriting my report, Dad reviewed it and said we needed to put a cover on it. So off we went to Woolworths, which was twenty minutes away in Indiana, Pennsylvania, to buy report covers for my report and stencils to print the title on it. I chose white folders. Dad was right; the unexpected details count. This little touch did elevate the report to the next level. I don't remember the grade I received.

Extra credit became an opportunity for me around every corner. In fourth grade when studying the westward movement of the US population, I decided I wanted to make a miniature replica of a covered wagon. I sketched it out and reviewed it with Dad. I was going to use coat hangers, cut to fit, as the bow supports for the wagon cover and one of my dad's handkerchiefs to replicate the canvas cover itself. But for the wagon, Dad told me we would need Uncle Mario to cut the wood for it on his saber saw. We went together to Bergman's Hardware to buy a scrap of plywood and then to Uncle Mario's home where he did the cutting according to my sketch and measurements. With the guiding hand of my dad, the covered wagon turned out quite nice for a fourth-grade project. But Dad insisted that I do as much of the work as I could, as the extra credit wasn't "extra credit" if he or Uncle Mario did it.

And when my mom's brothers and brothers-in-law were helping Uncle Mario put new shingles on the roof of his and Aunt Della's home, Dad was there. But Dad knew his strengths were not in laying the shingles; they weren't in using a saber saw either. So he stayed down from the roof and hoisted the packs of shingles and other roofing supplies up to his brothers-in-law.

This is not to say that Mom wasn't equally involved in the lives of my brother and me. She was, but in different, equally important ways. Mom and Dad's support intersected with our education and grades, however. Mom quizzed us every morning, during our grade school and early junior high school years, on the tests we were to have that day. She always checked our homework. When she had her own meetings to attend, Dad assumed the responsibilities. They never gave us answers though, but always pushed us to find the answers on our own.

Dad knew how to take command of his audience when giving speeches, whether he was serving as emcee for the tree-lighting ceremony of our town for the holiday season or standing in front of a large assembly of postmasters in a darkened, spotlighted hall or smaller assembly of volunteer firefighters and their spouses during their annual banquet at the Italian Club in Blairsville. He always walked to the podiums with a strong presence; he always stopped and deliberately looked over his audience once he reached the podium; he always seemed to know when to remove his glasses to make a point; he always looked straight at his entire audience when speaking; he always seemed to know how to hold his prepared speech, a speech he'd labored over on his typewriter in our home on Saturdays prior to his presentation. I know. I was there in the audience many times as a kid. So was my brother. And of course, my mom, ever the professional spouse.

As a couple, my parents knew how to work a room at an event or convention. They stopped to talk to everyone present. Everyone. I once asked Dad about this. He told me that it was a good practice professionally to shake everyone's hand in a room. Plus, people like to be recognized. Things I remember. Things I do.

At dinners in our home, after we said grace and blessed ourselves, our meal would begin. Mom and Dad first had their own chat. This was followed by the sometimes-ominous question, "How did you do on that test today?" And then Dad asked what we learned in school that day. Once, during my early junior high days, after learning the biological nature of reproduction, I was brimming over with excitement to tell Mom and Dad all about it. As I started, Dad gently said to me, "Rodney, that is not dinner conversation. We will talk about that later." Dinner conversation. I learned it had a level of appropriateness. I never forgot this.

And I remember when Dad and Mom took my brother and me to a function that Pat Stapleton, a Pennsylvania senator was to attend. Suited and with neckties properly tied in Dad's signature Windsor knot, we were given notice that we were going to be introduced. A quick conversation as to how to conduct ourselves was followed by observing Mom and Dad address Senator Stapleton, shaking hands, a kiss on Mom's cheek, exchanging a jovial moment, and initiating easy, familiar conversation. Dad then introduced me, followed by my younger brother. It was at this moment I learned, from watching Dad, the practice of constrained excitement. That is, the ability to not show emotion when your insides are a jiggling mess of anxiety and nerves.

***

There is much we learn when we don't know we are learning it during our formative years. These learnings seem to become natural ways of conducting our own lives later as adults. A handshake, a manner of having dinner conversation, the act of not showing emotions when your insides are jiggling while standing next to Diana Ross—an understanding of our own drives and limitations all form somewhere, sometime in our lives. They are all points of personal conduct registering as forms of personal per-fection that unknowingly accumulate in our young minds as we grow older. And then, one day, we see someone speaking or read of someone whose life sparks a recogni-tion of perfection, and they become role models for us in some way.

The recognition of this comes not from that moment of meeting them or reading about them. I believe it comes from what we learn in our formative years. A dad giving a speech, a mom checking our homework and nudging us to find the correct answers, a push here, an encourage-ment there, an oft-repeated phrase that becomes a quote we always remember. Our young minds were uncon-sciously observing and registering what our parents and other role models did and what they didn't do, but they still contributed through their own drives and despite limitations: I can't run a saber saw, but I can hoist shingles to a roof where my brothers-in-law will lay them.

Perhaps all this is what forms us without our knowing it at the time. But then, one day, we meet a Sally or read about an Irving, and we see elements in them which, for us, we identify as models, models of perfection.

But the perfection we are now seeing was seen and experienced and learned long before them.

Mistaken Identity

I arrived early to the late-afternoon Mass on a recent Thursday. Monsignor Sakano was the celebrant at the Chapel of the Sacred Hearts of Jesus and Mary that day, and when he arrived at the church, I asked him if he needed a lector for the Mass. He did, so I volunteered. The day was July 28, my brother's birthday.

After assisting Monsignor Sakano in setting up the altar for Mass and lighting the candles (a throwback to my days as an altar boy at Saint Bonaventure, my childhood church), I sat down in my usual seat: last row, on the aisle, left side of the church. There were only two other people present, as most don't show up until five to ten minutes before Mass begins. One was a professional, from New York University Hospital, who regularly attends daily Mass. One day, I will introduce myself to her and learn if she is a doctor, nurse, or a technician. She is one of those familiar people with whom we all exchange nods and smiles, but not necessarily conversations.

The other person was a stranger who sat distanced from the medical professional and me. The Chapel also serves as a chapel for both New York Medical Center and Bellevue Hospital, which are both located nearby. As a chapel, it is open during the day for private meditation for people from the hospital.

As I sat there, suddenly a very tall young man, probably in his early twenties, burst into the church. He darted across to the sacristy where Monsignor Sakano should have been, but apparently wasn't at that moment. After looking into the sacristy and waiting a few moments, the young man came to the center aisle, and walked midway down it. He was dressed in a Life Is Good tee and green-and-white, Hawaiian-inspired shorts. He carried an oversized and overly stuffed backpack on his back, the requisite accessory of college students. His eyes kept darting around the church.

The young man moved a little forward, then back. He then moved into a pew in front of the medical professional and sat down, his eyes still darting. Normally, my radar remains dormant. Living in New York City, though, you learn to have your radar ready to be engaged. You also learn to listen to your inner self, which I believe is your guardian angel. Most of the time, my radar is not needed, but with the recent gun violence in our country, sudden and unexpected movements by strangers causes me to now look but not look, be ready to react but appear calm, and remain steady...always steady.

Monsignor Sakano rang the bells to signal that he was entering the sanctuary to begin Mass. I couldn't help myself and kept looking over to the young man. As Mass progressed, he seemed to be fully engaged in the service, with hands clasped in a prayerful position during most of the service. I relaxed. Well, somewhat relaxed. His darting eyes troubled me.

After Mass, Karen, a friend of mine, and I cleared the altar for Monsignor Sakano. Returning the remaining water and wine, chalice, Mass books, and other items used by a priest during Mass, Karen, Monsignor Sakano, and I, as usual, engaged in a lively conversation. The day was sultry, the temperature was hot, and the humidity was high, making for an easy topic to start a conversation.

Monsignor Sakano is a very friendly man. His speech is staccato when not on the altar, but his homilies are presented in a measured voice spoken in the manner of your favorite college professor in your favorite class—the kind of delivery from a learned professor that would cause you to forget that you needed to take notes while you listened. He has eyes that sparkle like those of a new soul, a wide smile that is ever present, all set in the countenance of a priest whose time at the side of hospital beds far outnumber those times he spent conducting weddings, baptisms, and other celebratory occasions for his profession.

As the three of us were speaking, the young man with the backpack suddenly appeared in the doorway of the sacristy. Then, he stepped in. Karen, Monsignor Sakano, and I looked up at him, all a bit startled by the suddenness of his appearance. The young man had a look of panic on his face. The three of us stopped our conversation midsentence.

And then the young man said, "I was downtown at Saint Andrews, but the church was closed. I came up here because I heard this church was open. My mother is in the hospital. She needs prayers. She needs them now."

The young man's appearance was not one of panic. It was of desperation.

I looked at Monsignor Sakano. Compassion had suddenly softened his facial features, and his jovial demeanor in our conversation just a second prior was now one of priestly empathy. Karen and I looked at each other and departed, walking behind Monsignor Sakano as to not break his line of sight with the young man. They began talking as we walked out the door.

Karen and I had a brief, albeit nervously spoken, chat afterwards while standing in the back of the church. I inquired about the progress of her broken foot, now that the bandages were off; she told me she had to go to check on Siri, another parishioner whose dog was ill. We parted ways.

As I walked down Thirty-Third Street to return home, the tall young man was on my mind. I felt a catch in my throat as I imagined him holding his mother's hand as she lay in bed in a sterile hospital room. I thought of his feelings of desperation and perhaps aloneness in the moment. And I thought of that universal calm that suddenly and unexpectedly encompasses all of us during these moments, surrounding that desperation that still exists, but cradling us as we experience it.

Perhaps these moments are touched by our sense of the higher power of the universe to which we all belong, unsolicited, unexpected, but delivered deep within us when support is desperately needed, not unlike the out-stretched arm of our mother or father or sister or brother, husband or wife, partner or friend, minister or rabbi or priest—a universal arm thrust around our shoulders when emotions can no longer be held back.

Grandma Olson

Mom often told me that when I was old enough, I accompanied her and Dad on Sunday mornings to Saint Bonaventure Church; my young self had a fascination with the altar candles. I would point at them and exuberantly exclaim, "Birthday candles!" This would go on and on. Mom said she often had trouble quieting me as my excitement with the "birthday candles" grew. Finally, my parents decided I was too young and disruptive to attend Mass with them, so Dad stayed home with me while Mom went to church on Sundays and holidays.

Later in life, when my mind started to store places and events that I would remember, I recalled that Sunday mornings with my dad were a quiet time on Walnut Street, the street on which we lived. It was often called Church Street because at one end of it was the tan-brick Presbyterian church and at the other end, the white-clapboard Methodist church. Reverend Cooper and his wife lived in the two-story, burgundy-brick, Craftsman-style Presbyterian parsonage across the street from his church; Reverend Hempstead and his wife, Eleanor, lived in the two-story, Craftsman-style, burgundy-brick parsonage that sat next to the Methodist church. Even with all the Sunday-morning church traffic, I remember our street was always quiet on Sunday mornings. There was clearly a respect for the church services taking place at either end.

Mom sometimes spent part of her weekday afternoons watching me as I rode my red, pedal-driven firetruck up and down the sidewalk on our side of the street. I would pedal to the Presbyterian church and back. I liked to take the two sets of yellow ladders, which hung on each side of my firetruck, and place them on the cement steps leading up to the entrance of the Presbyterian church, pretending I was a fireman. I never climbed the ladders. Even then, I knew they could not support the weight of a young would-be volunteer fireman, a volunteer fireman like my dad. The firetruck had a bell attached to a string; I could ring it while seated. My childhood friend Dennis sometimes played with me on that firetruck as Mom watched while sharing afternoons with Dennis's mother, Fay, as young housewives did at that time in the last century. Coffee was usually involved.

Dad put a fence around the upper part of our terraced yard to "keep me in" when I was about that age. With my toy metal shovel in hand, Mom told me that I once dug myself out from under that fence. I was fascinated with the neighbor's doorbell and loved to ring it, repeatedly, as my innocent self stood outside of their front door. Mrs. Geary was always gentle with me—well, most of the time—when answering the door and explaining to me that I could not do this. I can still see her running to her front screen door on summer days, opening the screen door, crouching down and explaining, once again, that little boys do not ring doorbells. Perhaps this may be why my dad erected the fence around our yard at that time, the fence under which I dug myself out.

I loved the Gearys, especially their daughter, Kathy, who would take my young hand and escort me on hot summer days to the nearby confectionary, the Sugar Bowl, where she bought vanilla ice-cream cones for me and then patiently dealt with the drippy, sticky mess I became as I ate them.

Mom and Dad formed a lasting friendship with Reverend and Mrs. Hempstead. As a gift at my birth, they gave Mom and Dad an oak rocker that had been in one of their families for decades. I still have that rocker. It was an antique when Mom and Dad received it. I sometimes look at it and wonder what it was like when Mom rocked me as a baby while sitting in it, perhaps feeding a bottle to me of whatever newborns were fed back then. The rocker must carry many memories of both my family and the Hempstead generations as they found peace and comfort in its gentle rocking while contemplating life and world events over its long expanse of existence. The rocker now has my memories in it.

Reverend and Mrs. Hempstead hosted us at their home at Christmas. Dad dressed in a suit, Mom in her Sunday finest. Mom dressed me in a suit, complemented by a bow tie, and bundled me into my grey-tweed dress coat with matching cap and earmuffs. Mom always put earmuffs on me, and my knit gloves were always attached to my tweed coat by mitten clips.

We then walked across the street and were "received" at the side door of the parsonage. I was given strict rules from Mom and Dad beforehand: "Only speak when spoken to," "Sit and be calm," "Do not get up from your chair unless you ask permission," and so on. I always obeyed. Why tempt fate?

We sat in "the parlor." At Christmas, Reverend and Mrs. Hempstead always had a beautifully decorated evergreen to the left of their fireplace. My assigned seat was a large wingback chair to the right of the fireplace. After asking, I was permitted to jump down from the chair (my feet didn't touch the floor) and observe the tree up close. I remember, once, peering into the dining room, but was quickly reminded to return to my chair.

And there I sat until Mrs. Hempstead, now in a holiday apron, offered me a cookie on a holiday-motif china plate. She then served coffee to Mom, Dad, and Reverend Hempstead from a coffee service, complete with matching china cups and saucers, creamer and sugar bowl, and linen napkins. In hindsight, this was all from another era, perhaps a more genteel time in the twentieth century. After the coffee was served and a cookie tray presented to the adults, Mrs. Hempstead offered me a small glass of milk.

Later in the year, Mom and Dad reciprocated the Hempsteads' invitation. They arrived in their Sunday best; we were likewise dressed in ours. We sat in our "living room." Mom donned a pink, ruffled floral apron as she served coffee and pastries, all made with her own hands, creations such as nut rolls, nut horns, perhaps apricot rolls, fig cookies, and decorated sugar cookies. In my own home, I was given the same rules as those issued when we visited Reverend and Mrs. Hempstead. The Hempsteads were both gracious, soft-spoken, ever-smiling people with deep-rooted souls calmed by their faith. They seemed to enjoy time with me, and memories of them and their smiles still echo softly in my mind.

I didn't understand at the time the connection the Olson family had to the Methodist church in my hometown of Black Lick. Grandma started attending when she and Granddad moved to Marshall Heights, a suburb of Black Lick. Their family of ten children was still young. Grandma was always devoted to her faith and to her church. Uncle John, in his written history of my Olson family, said that Grandma walked to church each Sunday with her ten children. They entered the church in single file, led by Grandma, my dad and his sister Ruth, the two oldest, bringing up the rear. It was during one of the Olson entrances that teenage Uncle John first noticed the beautiful Ruth Olson. He wrote in the family history that he fell in love with her at that moment. Eventually, they started dating and after college, married. Aunt Ruth often stated later in life that "John was the only love of my life."

Grandma started stopping by our home on Sunday mornings before church. With Mom at Saint Bonaventure services, Grandma once offered to take me to the Methodist church with her. Dad was okay with it and dressed me for church. After this, I started going to church with Grandma on Sunday mornings while we lived in the house on Walnut Street. I sat reverently next to Grandma, sometimes leaning against her. Sometimes she walked me to the "annex" of the church to attend Sunday school while church services were held. It was there that I learned the song "Jesus Loves Me." To this day, it reminds me of Grandma Olson.

The Olson history with the Black Lick Methodist Church lasted a lifetime. My dad's youngest sisters, Helen and Joyce, were married there. Both beautiful brides, on each of their wedding days, Aunt Helen and Aunt Joyce dressed in our home and were escorted across the street by my tuxedoed dad when their ceremonies were to begin. I imagine they were stunning as they appeared in their wedding gowns, slowly descending the stairs from our second floor to the landing between floors, stopping then turning left on the landing, and finally slowly proceeding down the long flight of stairs to the vestibule of our home. I was too young to remember these moments in person, but I have my parents' black-and-white photos of those days, which paint the picture. The Methodist church became the family church of some of my dad's nine siblings.

Mom and Dad were comfortable with my attending both the Methodist church with Grandma and eventually (when the candles held less of an interest) Saint Bonaventure when I was young. I was baptized, confirmed, and am a practicing Roman Catholic, but I am also very comfortable attending services in the Methodist church, and for that matter, most Protestant services. Mom would often say, "There is only one God." I now understand her saying came with the corollary "There are many ways of worshipping God and many paths to Him."

As humans, we are fortunate to have brains that act in a manner much like motion-picture cameras, taking in all the events of our lives and recording them on their own form of film. Unfortunately, the sound systems don't record as clearly as the images, and the film does fade as time goes by. But, still, there are vivid segments of that film that remain clear in our brains throughout our lives. Perhaps both consciously reliving the fading moments in our thoughts and retelling the stories of the past help to keep the memories from fading. It is important. Like those old black-and-white movies that Hollywood strives each year to restore, many of our memories are too precious to be lost…

…like my leaning against my grandma Olson while sitting with her in her pew in the Methodist Church.

Impressions

Although I have lived in New York City for over forty years now, I still receive a morning email from the *Indiana Gazette*, the local newspaper from the area of Western Pennsylvania in which I was born and raised. I always read the headlines. Now they are of people I only occasionally recognize. The places are all familiar, but look different after forty years. I was a paperboy for this same newspaper when my uncle Bob was employed by the paper; it was then known as the *Indiana Evening Gazette*. It is another moment for "you can take the boy out of Black Lick, but you can't take Black Lick out of the boy."

My dad's ritual on coming home from work was to read the headlines of *The Gazette*, as we called it, in his easy chair. We'd then have dinner, after which Dad would retire to his chair again and "read the paper" until the early evening news came on the television. I often heard the rustling of the pages of the paper as Dad turned them or the quiet snapping of pages as he straightened them. Meanwhile, I was busy helping Mom clear the table and wash and dry the dinner dishes. My little brother, "the baby," was always excused from these duties, even when he was old enough, in my mind, to help me.

Mom and Dad always perused the obituaries. I never thought much of this as they discussed people they knew personally or with whom they were acquainted. Those people were a generation or two ahead of them for many years, then they became contemporaries of my parents; some of the names and faces I also knew. Life moves forward like this for all of us.

I now read the obituaries of the *Indiana Gazette* each day, as my parents did. This past week, I read that Joann passed. The photo of her in the online paper was as I knew her from forty-plus years ago. She was the mother of my high school classmate Mike. I Googled the funeral home in which her services were to be held and read the tributes posted for her; every tribute spoke of the beauty of the woman, the mother of my classmate, I once knew.

***

After graduating from high school, my summer lawn-mowing career of the past five years had not generated enough money for me to contribute to my upcoming college education. I don't know when or why I did this, but I went to the former Regency Mall in Indiana, Pennsylvania, and completed an application for employment with Montgomery Ward. It may have been due to my friend and classmate, Leda, working there, but the memory eludes me. Leda was quick to rise to a manager position with Montgomery Ward. I was offered a job, accepted, and was glad to have Leda there to spend some time with during my summer lunch breaks.

My mom's cousin Emma worked at Montgomery Ward during this time. Mom's father, my pap, and Emma's father, Great-Uncle Pete, were brothers. I wonder as I write this, years later, if Emma had anything to do with my hiring. Nonetheless, it was comforting to have my cousin once removed there with me. When our shifts ended at the same time, I sometimes gave Emma a ride to her home in my blue-and-white Maverick. In the area I was raised, the concept of six degrees of separation was more like three degrees of separation. Someone knows someone; someone is always related.

I was assigned to Ruth, who was the manager of the catalog division. My job was to manage the catalog stockroom for her. She gave me the tour, the instructions, her expectations, and my schedule. I also had to keep the stockroom floor swept. I had a desk with a light above it in a darkened stockroom. I was happy. The loss of the great tans from mowing lawns each summer day was worth the sacrifice for larger paychecks.

Ruth was an older, no-nonsense kind of woman. Impeccably dressed each day, she ran a very strict operation. A place for everything and everything in its place. Every morning, trunks arrived full of customer orders in labeled plastic bags. My job was to check in the orders within a given amount of time and file them on the rows of shelves in the darkened stockroom. When customers arrived to pick up their packages, Ruth would signal for me to retrieve the package and hand it to her at the counter.

One morning, I arrived to find on the central floor of the stockroom all the packages from the shelves in a pile almost as high as I was tall. Ruth had decided on a new method of organizing them. My job was to restock the rows and rows of shelves using her new organizational method. Let me state again, the packages were stacked almost as high as I was tall on the stockroom floor.

I learned to love working for Ruth. And I learned to love her and her way of doing business. After that first summer, she hired me back at Christmas and then during consecutive summers and holidays. Apparently she liked my work, and she liked me. One summer, she told me to come to work wearing nicer clothes, that she wanted me to substitute at times for her at the customer counter. I had to look nice to be in front of the public. She taught me to use the cash register. She taught me to use the credit card machine. I was given personal goals for opening Montgomery Ward credit-card accounts. This was a real incentive, as I received monetary rewards based on the number of accounts I opened. And I had to remain looking nice while still working in that darkened stockroom and still sweeping the floors.

As time went on, I needed more money for school. One summer, I took on a second job at Weston's, another department-store retailer nearby. I would leave Ruth at five each day, run to McDonald's for a double cheeseburger (I ate so many that summer that I still can't stomach the smell of them after all these years), and change from my nice clothes into stock-boy clothes by six, when I started my work at Weston's. My changing room was the bathroom of a gas station situated between Montgomery Ward and Weston's. Yep, you read that right!

I finished work at ten each night and started again by nine the next morning with Ruth. This bought my books for school, among other necessities.

Grad school brought the need for even more money for my education. When a classmate told me he was taking a two-week course in bartending to make more money for school, I decided to join him. Mom and Dad were okay with the cost of the course, which they generously agreed to pay. So on returning home that summer, I continued to work for Ruth during the day and was fortunate to land a bartending job at Chestnut Ridge Inn on the Green. I say fortunate since it was the local country club and prestigious in its own right.

I was well acquainted with Chestnut Ridge Inn on the Green. Two of my mom's brothers were instrumental in its development, a cousin was a chef there, and Dad, together with Frank, another local postmaster, hosted many, many Pennsylvania Postmaster Golf Outings at Chestnut Ridge. And Dad golfed there regularly.

So I worked for Ruth during the day; changed into black pants, a white shirt, and a black vest; and by seven or so, began tending bar until one or two in the morning. Then, I was back with Ruth by nine the next morning. Looking back, I am grateful for the energy of youth.

George was the manager of the restaurant and bar at Chestnut Ridge. He was the brother-in-law of the owner. George's wife, Verneta, was hostess. Like Ruth, George was strict in his reign over the restaurant and bar. I learned his ways and expectations within the first week of employment. The restaurant was elegant, exquisitely designed and decorated, and architecturally unique, with a black-glass and dark-wood bar in an L shape, which made it easy to maneuver and serve customers, its brass countertop easy to keep clean. The bar had a door which conveniently opened to the kitchen for when I ran low on lemons, limes, and other garnishes.

It was here that I met Joann. She was a waitress at Chestnut Ridge Inn on the Green and had worked there for several years prior to my arrival. At first, I did not know she was Mike's mother. At first, however, I did know I liked her.

Joann was always impeccably dressed. Her posture was perfect. Her personality drew you in, made you comfortable, permitted you to listen as she attentively listened to you. She always had a warm and welcoming smile. She was a very easy partner in work. During my first week, when we had downtime and I was alone behind the bar, she came over and explained to me how to "work for tips." I didn't realize at that time, nor was it taught to me in my bartending course, that I had to "work for tips." It was the tips that were important. Boy, was Joann right.

Joann gave me the entry-level pointers for tips: smile, listen, engage with customers who were alone at the bar, compliment women on how they looked. Back then, the big one was to always light the cigarette of a woman at the bar while looking at them. Yes, I was "working for tips," but I know there was more to this, as the customers with whom I engaged did appreciate the attention. Perhaps that was the reason they were there—a little attention, a moment away from real life, a few hours of relaxation in the luxury of a beautiful bar and restaurant in a country club while socializing with the strangers sitting next to them…or with the bartender.

I had fun with and really appreciated Joann. I still remember her coming to the bar after initially greeting guests at their tables and taking their drink orders. Sometimes she put one elbow on the waitress station at the bar, looked at me sideways while kinda smirking, and gave me the drink orders. Other times she was in a rush and speed spoke the orders to me in rapid succession so she could get to her next table. But she always did so while smiling. I remember, too, that she liked the special garnishes I put on drinks. When the pineapple and maraschino cherries in the silhouette of a parrot, which I made for piña coladas, weren't there, she reminded me and waited for me to sculpt the parrot. Sometimes when I was swamped with customers and waitress orders, she reached behind the bar for the fruit and created her own special sculptures.

Mom and Dad often frequented Chestnut Ridge Inn for various functions, so they knew Joann. I think it was Dad who told me she was Mike's mom. I worked the bar once when Dad and Frank held one of their Postmaster Golf Outings. It was a lucrative afternoon. I had to ask Ruth for the day off from my work with her at Montgomery Ward to tend bar for the golf outing; Ruth understood completely my reason for this. I must admit I was proud to be my dad's son behind the bar that day.

The bar work, however, wasn't always the easiest. There were George's standards to meet and the need to always be prepared for surprise visits from restaurant inspectors. And sometimes I had to deal with unpleasant customers. Once, a large group of boisterous men from Johnstown wrapped themselves around the U-shaped end of the bar. After many rounds of drinks, they left, leaving only a dime on the counter. I wanted to follow them to the door, tell them they forgot something, and hand the dime back to them. I didn't.

Another time, I had a customer who demanded another drink when I knew I had to cut him off. We kept the extra glassware under the far end of the bar, partially out of the sight of customers, but still somewhat visible. When I explained to him I could not serve him another drink, he started yelling, got up, and threw the remainder of his current drink at the clean glassware under the counter. Security quickly escorted him out of the back of the restaurant, through the delivery entrance. I had a mess to clean after he was thrown out.

I don't remember many people I knew coming to Chestnut Ridge Inn on the Green while I was bartending. It seemed that mostly we hosted out-of-town guests. I do remember my dad's youngest sister, Helen, and her husband, Bob, coming once to celebrate something. I remember Aunt Helen being wrapped in her fur jacket and looking beautiful that evening. And their daughter, my cousin Linda…

One evening, Linda showed up at the bar nicely dressed and somewhat underage for sitting at a bar. She said she just stopped by to see me. Like any good cousin, I made her a piña colada, complete with the pineapple parrot. She sat for an hour or so nursing her drink while we talked and then departed.

George came over to me after Linda departed to inquire about the young woman to whom I was paying so much attention. I was sure I was busted for serving a minor. Not sure where this was all going, I mumbled something, and he then said that she was quite pretty and asked if "my friend" could bring some of her girlfriends to the bar on occasion; they needed some pretty young women frequenting the bar to attract more young men. With the vivid image of Aunt Helen chasing me down Route 22 with a pitchfork, I calmly replied to George, "I'll see what I can do."

Reading Joann's obituary brought many memories back about her, about that time in my life, about Ruth, and about Mom and Dad and their support for me during my education.

Joann left an impression on me, an impression that to this day resides in a special place in my brain that, once reactivated, brings with it a flood of related memories about a woman who took me under her wing as a newly minted bartender, about a supervisor who was tough as nails on the outside but a heart of gold on the inside, and about a time in life that I didn't realize then was so special and so good to me.

It really was.

Edgemont

Joni and I grew up together in the same neighborhood, the Edgemont section of my hometown of Black Lick, Pennsylvania. Her family lived on my block in a stately, two-story, 1920s or 1930s, red-brick home that had a wide front porch designed for leisurely sitting on warm summer evenings and an interior complemented by beautiful woodwork and a grand staircase. Joni's childhood home must have been the first on the block when most of the area of Edgemont was being developed from farmland, a neighborhood dominated still by the original farmhouse in which the mother of my friend Becky still resides. I can still see and hear Joni's graceful mother, in her gentle voice, calling for Joni from their back porch while we were all playing.

Like many childhood friends, I had lost track of Joni when I moved to New York City after graduate school. Our high school class had maybe two reunions. I only attended one and departed at 9:00 p.m. after saying hello to most of my former classmates. Some of us are once again connected through the addictive mysteries of Facebook. There is another reunion scheduled for later this year. The two digits comprising the anniversary of it leave me in disbelief.

Joni was part of our large neighborhood of Edge-mont kids. We were all products of the mid- to early 1960s, our parents mostly of the Greatest Generation produced during World War II. And most of our parents were friends. Joni had an older brother, Tim, and a younger brother, Alan. Adding to our gang were Joey, Tina, and Susie; the Twins, Doug and Dave, with their older sister Janice, and brother Jack; Jeannie, who lived up the street and one block over from the rest of us; and Brenda, who lived next to Joni. Joni, Joey, Janice, and I were all the same age and living on the same block. In fact, Joey, Janice, and I were all in Mrs. Gahagan's first-grade classroom.

One block to the right of us were my cousin Marla, Becky, my lifelong friend Rita, and her brother, Gene. There was also Rita and Gene's cousin Brucie who was blessed with red hair and freckles, one of those iconic red-headed kids that every neighborhood had back then. In third grade, Brucie made an anatomically correct woman in art class and was hauled off the principal's office for it; we all heard him screaming and crying down the hall, "That's the way my mom looks!" I am sure Brucie went on to become a renowned sculptor.

There were Teddy, Donny, and Randy, who lived up the hill from all of us. And there were my cousins Karen and her brother, Frankie, who lived across the street from me. Both were a little older than the rest of us. Karen was a majorette in high school, thus making her the envy and idol of many of the younger neighborhood girls who secretly watched her practice baton twirling in her backyard. Later, during junior high, another family built a beautiful, blond-brick 1960s ranch-style home next to Jeannie's family home, bringing Bobbie and her sister, Judy, to our neighborhood. Oh, and Penny Sue appeared as a special treat each year when, for most of the summer, she visited with her grandparents from her home in Eastern Pennsylvania.

As kids, we all played together over the years. But the play evolved as we grew older. Our pickup Wiffleball games in Joey and Tina's backyard are a significant memory for me. Joni was always there with us, together with our yellow-plastic bats and white-plastic Wiffle balls that stung if they hit you with enough force. Summers found the girls playing with their dolls or board games on the front porches.

We boys worked on tree houses that never were finished, played with our Tonka trucks, and took lots of hikes, always mindful of poison ivy as we walked through the forested areas nearby. Sometimes we did a bike hike to a nearby lake, only to return home with bottles of frog eggs to watch morph into tadpoles and return them later to the lake. Our moms sometimes packed a lunch for us to have along the way. We were comfortable knocking unexpectedly on the doors of our friends' homes, asking if they could come out and play. Sometimes during play, the moms invited us in for lunch, always with a phone call to our own moms to inform them we were being fed.

We rode our bikes everywhere, often congregating at the playground area of Burrell Elementary School, which we all attended. The playground had three sets of slides, swings, and seesaws, all of different sizes for the various age ranges attending the school. And it had a merry-go-round and a set of monkey bars, on which we hung upside down. If we fell, we hit the dirt underneath. There was no rubber padding. Sometimes we made the merry-go-round spin so fast that some of us flew off. Once Jack swung so high on a swing that he amazed us by going over the top. Yes, this is all an insurance nightmare today.

Autumns found us with large paper bags from the grocery stores, scouring the local cornfields after the harvest was completed and gathering as much discarded field corn as we could carry. After shucking, we threw the hardened kernels as "tricks" at the front porches of homes on Halloween. The once-shingled homes now covered in aluminum siding were always the best to hit. And deer season brought intrigue as to whose father or uncle shot a deer and how many "points" the antlers had. Some of us watched in amazement the skinning and butchering process; some of us didn't. Hunting rifles were then locked away until the next year. I once watched Joey's dad teach young Joey how to skin a few rabbits that he shot during rabbit season. Joey's dad offered a rabbit tail to me. I declined.

All of Edgemont was on a gentle sloping hill. Joni's yard was the best for sled riding when we were permitted to use it. Otherwise, we went to the top of Catalpa Street, put lookouts at the intersections, and off we went, lying belly down on our sleds. Cars did stop for us kids as we wildly swung our arms to signal "stop" at those intersections on snowy winter days as one or more of us zipped by on our sleds. We repeated the same with our homemade go-carts during the summers.

And play wasn't always of our own making. Mrs. Shields, a retired grade school teacher who lived between our home and Joey's, sometimes invited the neighborhood boys for lunch and to play games or do crafts. Once, she taught us how to weave Easter baskets out of construction paper. She had colorful Easter grass and jelly beans for us to put into each completed basket. She did the same with the girls in our neighborhood, but since boys weren't invited to these luncheons, I don't know what they did or made.

Mrs. Shields, too, had an upright piano that she played for us while we sang along. On summer mornings, she and her husband, Dick, had breakfast at a table for two in their backyard, complete with a tablecloth and linen napkins. That same table hosted their afternoon four-o'clock teas, complete with a china teapot, cups, and saucers. And summer and autumn evenings found them sitting on their wide, covered front porch, talking leisurely while rocking on their porch swing. Sometimes we stopped by on our bikes to say, "Hello, Mrs. Shields! Hello, Mr. Shields!"

Why this reminiscing on my childhood neighborhood? It was the foundation for us kids from Edgemont back then. And in hindsight, many with whom I am still connected via Facebook now call it magical. Perhaps it was, but we did not know it at that time. For us, it just "was." We made a lot of good memories.

Well, not all were good. There was the time Joey and I dammed a ditch that was on the street side of a sidewalk in front of his home. We dammed it to make a lake for our Tonka-truck village. The ditch did fill up with water after a heavy rain. We were thrilled. The dammed water, however, backed up into the basement of Joey's home. It wasn't a pretty scene for Joey and me when his dad returned home from work that day.

Well, then there was the day Joey and I felt sad for his father's two male beagles he used during hunting season. The two beagles were always kept separated from each other. Joey and I thought they should be permitted to play together, like us, and we released them together into a fenced area in Joey's backyard. I can still see Joey's mom running out of the house and down the back steps to break up the fracas. This was one of the times Joey's dad may have suggested to Joey and me that we should not play together for a period of time. How did we know?

The neighborhood parents watched out for all of us. If one of us fell and skinned a knee while playing in a friend's yard, his or her mother consoled us, stopped our crying, cleaned the wound, and bandaged the knee. Our parents, too, were not short on disciplining us as a group or even individually if we did something that was, let's say, out of line. I believe our parents appreciated this; they didn't get angry with each other over it.

I am not sure that our neighborhood's type of magic still exists for kids. There was no technology to distract us. We didn't need to fear being out and about, playing in the neighborhood together. Or riding our bikes everywhere. And we all knew that we had to be home by dinnertime. This was a nonnegotiable.

Sunday mornings found us all at our respective churches. There were no Sunday-morning sporting events that kept us from church; no washing was ever hung on a clothesline on Sundays (except for the cloth diapers on the clotheslines for families with newborns), no washing of cars or cutting of grass either. Our two-week summer religion classes were a requirement.

We all seemed to sit down for Sunday midday dinners after our church services. Joey's family visited his grandparents. So did Joni's. My grandma Olson sometimes visited us or had midday dinner with us after attending the Methodist church services. We then visited relatives. For my family, my mom's parents had gone on to their next life before I was born. In their place, Mom always insisted we visit with her oldest sibling, my uncle Pete and his wife, Aunt Dolly, on Sundays. He became the family patriarch. When he passed, the mantel went to my aunt Giggi, second in line among my mom's siblings. We always seemed to visit with her and her husband, my uncle Miller, then. Visiting families on Sundays took precedent over televised sports. Well, except for when the Pirates were in the World Series or the Steelers in the Super Bowl.

On our televisions in the evenings, we had scenes from the Vietnam War, Civil Rights, and Women's Rights movements and marches, serious inequality, the Watts and Newark riots, three major assassinations (our neighborhood went quiet during the mourning period for President John F. Kennedy, who was a contemporary of our parents), and, earlier on, the Cold War. In grade school, we learned to "duck and cover" under our desks for atomic-bomb drills in addition to our regularly scheduled fire drills. We also ducked under the sills of the large windows in our classrooms because, as Mrs. Gahagan said, the shards of glass would blow over us as the windows imploded from an atomic bomb.

But our neighborhood seemed to insulate us from these traumas. The peace and tranquility of playing with our friends, feeling safe in our neighborhood and protected by all our surrounding parents, was a gift that we did not realize we had back then. And as neighborhood friends, we learned to trust each other and to lean into each other, to share secrets and keep them, and protect and watch out for each other and our younger siblings. Surely, I believe all of us can say that, together with the upbringing provided by our parents, this gave us a place of calmness and security that developed within our inner beings and perhaps remains with all of us today. And in some way, perhaps because of Facebook, we still share. I know I can tap into mine, and I now, in later life, know from where it originated.

Carol

I met Carol when she was a buyer for Liz Claiborne Outlets, and I was head of planning and allocation for the retail division of Liz Claiborne. Every few months, we met and discussed transfers of the retail division's excess inventory. Carol negotiated the pricing the outlet division would pay for our excess product.

Later, we worked more closely on what is known as a "hierarchy conversion" (don't trouble yourself with understanding this retail-specific process), and on a system upgrade, configuration, and installation. Unfortunately, I remember the hierarchy work vividly. During it, I was developing a very detailed structure of naming and sequential numbering while on a flight to Los Angeles. I was doing the work in ink on pads of white, college-ruled paper. As I was diligently developing numbering schematics, my seatmate, a businessman who, like me, was dressed in a suit, had a moment of drama about something unknown to me. He suddenly waved his left hand in a flourish, and as he did, he knocked his cup of coffee onto my pad of very detailed work. It was soaked. All was lost. I reacted. A flight attendant came rushing down the aisle. I explained in a heavily constrained voice what just had happened to my hours and hours of work.

The flight attendant suggested that she and I walk to the back of the plane so I could let go of some energy. I accompanied her. She was a calming voice in a sea of Italian and Scandinavian-Irish rage within me. She later accompanied me back to my seat, where my seatmate could not stop apologizing. It was all an accident and an act of fate. Perhaps the second outcome of the naming and numbering schematic was meant to be better than the first. I don't remember.

Upon arrival in LA late that night, I checked into my hotel. As I started to unpack after the trauma of the flight, the hotel power suddenly went out, taking with it the air-conditioning on a hot Los Angeles summer night. It never came back on until the next day. The window in the room was sealed shut. I slept that night with my hotel door open to allow airflow into the room.

Perhaps it was her work on the system upgrade, configuration, and installation that ignited a fire in Carol to evolve her career drive and passions to the system side of retail, and away from the product side. Her decision put her in an enviable and very knowledgeable position with a highly sought-after skill set that combined product knowledge with systems knowledge. She later enhanced her degree with project-management certification.

I came to admire Carol and her strive for excellence while working together at Liz. I liked that we could laugh together at the mundane and absurdity that is often present in working environments. I liked that we connected.

Later, I moved on from Liz. I was never happy there after Liz Corporate moved our offices from the convenience of New York City to Secaucus, New Jersey, a morning bus ride away and up to a two-hour bus ride home during rush hour in the evenings through the Lincoln Tunnel. Additionally, the area was swarmed by mosquitos during the summers. We watched them pulsating, thick on the office windows, crazy to get through to all of us, their desired victims. So the career move for me was the right thing. Carol and I lost contact after this, as happens with many close-working relationships during one's career when someone leaves a job.

I decided to leave retail proper a few years later. After several weeks with a career counselor and multiple personality tests, she suggested consulting as a career option for me in light of my years of experience on the numbers side of retail and my degree in finance. I honestly could not think of a worse career move, as I disliked most of the consultants I had been forced to work with over the years.

But Sally, my former CEO at Ann Taylor, called one day and told me about one of the retailers for which she served on the board of directors. The retailer wanted to eventually file an IPO and needed directional help in the management of their largest investment—their inventory. After Sally reminded me of my lack of current cash flow, I decided it was a good idea to give this consulting opportunity a try.

Fast-forward two years later, the retailer was bought by another larger retail organization. By now, I was firmly and happily entrenched in consulting, and Kim and I had formed our consulting partnership. I was asked by our client, the smaller retailer, to assist in the cutover of the process and systems to the larger retailer after the purchase was completed. My client gave me a lot of direction as to what to expect when first meeting the CEO, CFO, CIO, and technical team who were engineering and executing the cutover of the larger retailer. I was a little nervous, but eager to do the work. I wasn't all that familiar with the larger retailer and, honestly, did not know what to expect.

I arrived at my client's office the morning of the initial series of meetings and was ushered into a conference room. As soon as the door closed behind me, from the other side of the room, I heard, "Rod!" Up jumped Carol from her seat. She raced over to me and gave me a big hug. I could not believe what was happening. I remember looking at her and asking if she was part of this process. This was kind of a stupid question, in hindsight, on my part. Why else would Carol have been there? But Carol said she was part of the cutover process and now worked in the systems area of the larger retailer. We didn't have time for catch-up conversation then, but during the meeting, I learned that Carol and I, together, would lead the cutover project. Estimated timing: twelve months.

So Carol and I began our work and our professional friendship again. We were partnered with Melody, a great manager from the systems vendor we were using. The three of us worked closely together for months, moving through many solutions, many requirements, many unknowns, many formal meetings to report progress, many anxieties, and many laughs, many dinners, many drinks (but not too many), and many nights and days of sheer exhaustion. Melody was traveling to and from Toronto to Florida. I was commuting weekly to Florida from New York. We completed the cutover in nine months; three months shy of the projected twelve-month timing.

And so, as time progressed, Carol became the IT liaison for my former client, the smaller purchased company, and I was offered an opportunity to step away from my consulting practice and join the smaller, now-purchased company. I was informed that I would be in charge of operations, budgeting, planning and allocation, production and sourcing, technical design, quality, and a lot of other areas of the business. Including systems—I would continue to work with Carol. I accepted. Kim kept our consulting practice moving forward, but without me.

Life moves on, and Carol departed this company; later, so did I. By now, our professional friendship had transitioned to a personal friendship. We were never too far apart to pick up the phone and have a chat. Later in our careers, Carol and I partnered again to assist a private equity firm in the purchase of yet another retailer. Carol focused on the due diligence for the technical infrastructure and systems, then wrote and presented to potential investors an exhaustive review and road map for upgrading the systems environment. Later, when the company decided to move its offices 120 miles away to a more urban location, Carol engineered the complete systems move, including dismantling and moving nine computer servers, installing and restarting them within eleven hours. I loved that Carol had them accompanied over the road by a security force to protect the company's data stored within the servers.

So one day my business partner, Kim, and I were looking through some of my mom and dad's photo albums during some downtime from our work. I don't remember why we decided to do this, but it was a break that both of us needed at that moment. When I turned to the wedding photo of my parents, Kim said, "Carol looks like your mom."

As I often say, the world stopped its rotation for a moment for me.

I looked again…and again. I registered Carol's face in my brain and transferred it to my mom's face, which in that photo was adorned and framed by her wedding veil cascading down from the sequined crown to which it was attached. Yep, the same features. Not quite the same face, but yes, the same features.

My mind then paused.

I had to get back to work. But the moment stayed with me. Kim will often say that she is always right. I'm not sure she is joking. Most of the time, I will agree with her because she is right. Kim has a way of seeing things straight through the middle, straight to the core of what she is reviewing or analyzing. It is a gift. She is very smart.

But, later, I wondered why I had never made this association between Mom and Carol. Carol and I by now had known each other for at least twenty years. To this day, I am still amazed that I never made this recognition. I wanted to tell Carol, but I also wanted to wait. I had to digest it all and make sense of all the multiple layers and dimensions that this presented to me.

But then, maybe, I wasn't meant to see the resemblance until Kim did. Maybe I wasn't ready for this understanding until that day. But, apparently, I was meant to understand it at some point in life because kismet brought Carol and me together again that one morning years ago in a conference room for a meeting.

There are friendships we form in life that appear out of nowhere. Some develop and then diminish. Some simply move on. But what of those that stick? The relationships that form and grow deeper, where commonalities are realized and shared, where interests grow simultaneously, where an ease forms and never moves off the mark, where disagreements are surpassed by understanding, are unique.

Friendships that form that have these baselines, but where it is later realized that one of the friends resembles the other's parent or sibling, aunt or uncle—what of those?

I often wonder if the life we are in now is not the only life we have lived. Do our souls have the opportunity to take on different bodies over different times and return to this world or another? Are our souls asked by our higher power to return to earth with the knowledge we gained from a past life and live another life in another body during another time to assist someone or something that can benefit from our previous knowledge, talents, and / or experiences?

Before the revelation by Kim, I often joked with her that we were married in another life. We have a lot in common, share synergies, and can argue, as people have said, like a married couple. But over forty-plus years now, we have stuck together as business partners and personal friends. People have often called me her "work husband" and Kim, my "work wife." But I do often wonder if our souls knew each other in another life. Our commonalities and synergies are intriguing to me. Perhaps we were once married in another life during another age, perhaps in another location in the universe.

It took me a long time to mention to Carol the resemblance that she has to my mother. I first needed to understand it from deep within my being. And I wanted to tell her, but had an uneasiness about it. Yet I knew I needed to do it.

I wondered why I felt such an uneasiness about this impending conversation. Was Mom signaling down from heaven that she didn't want me to tell Carol? Was I crossing a line of universal understanding that was not meant to be crossed? Was the reality of what I was about to tell Carol just too much for my mind and soul to digest? Was I just being nervous about nothing?

But I eventually did tell Carol. The moment was a light one. We agreed that we probably were either related in this life or brother and sister in another one. A random cluster of genes shared between us is not unreasonable given the Mediterranean ancestry of my mom and Carol's parents.

Carol has moved on from retail. She works with Robert, her longtime boyfriend from Italy, in his business. They visit with his family back in Italy, but when doing so, will spend a month or longer with them. I am a little envious that they can spend so much time in Italy, a country I have come to love, a country whose DNA I share. Maybe someday I will have the time to do so.

And maybe someday I will understand the connection Carol and I share…

Carol, my friend who has a striking resemblance to my mother…

…and so, there I sat very early one Sunday morning, waiting to board my plane at JFK when, *out of the blue*, I was compelled to send Carol a text. She replied and asked me if I had a moment to talk. I did. She called. She then told me that her mother had just passed away.

She had *just* passed away.

Necessities

I was in an office-supply store today. It is a place that my business partner, Kim, and I can lose ourselves in for hours. It must be a holdover from our time as kids in toy stores. Or in the cereal aisle of a grocery store.

I was there to return used ink cartridges from my printer for recycling. And I needed sticky notes. I found myself comparing prices on sticky notes, which is something I always do. I believe they are unreasonably expensive. The private-label brand offered twelve tablets for $21.99. The brand name offered eighteen tablets for $23.99. I went with the brand name. They were a more vibrant yellow in color and clearly a better deal.

At the checkout counter, a lovely young woman greeted me. She asked me to type my phone number into a keypad for the rewards program that I have with this office supply store. I love rewards programs and tend to carry all my rewards-program cards with me during errands. Hey, you never know where you may find a great deal! After handing her my rewards card, once scanned, the price of the $23.99 brand-name sticky notes appeared as $17.99 on the POS screen. *Wow,* I thought, *one dollar per tablet. What a buy!* I enthusiastically expressed this to the young woman. She agreed.

After doing so, I wondered, *Why do I need these?* Years ago, I lived a life without these. Why do I need them now? I just paid a little under twenty dollars (with taxes) for something that was never part of my earlier life, during which I lived nicely without them. Actually, I had no concept of ever needing anything like this back then.

I took my purchase and departed the office-supply store. I felt good about the promotional price I received. I was still wondering, though, why I needed the sticky notes that were now in a bag I was carrying with me. And when did I realize that I first needed them? I was carrying that bag of newly purchased sticky notes with me as I embarked on my morning two-mile walk, which I try to do each morning to start my day.

I found my mind suddenly consumed with things in my life that I wondered if I truly needed. And if I did, when did that desire suddenly become a need? How much of my consumerism today was not present years ago, during a period of my life in which I seemed to manage nicely without those current needs?

And that made me think of texting. I never needed it until it was suddenly there. Why do I need it now? Prior to its invention, my life was fine without it. I suspect so were other lives.

Texting has brought years of anxiety with it, anxiety which began its takeover of our lives when email was first introduced. The assumed sense of absolute urgency to read and respond to a text upon hearing the ping of your cell phone or seeing a message pop up on its screen has taken over all forms of calmness and ease in a day.

Ping! Respond! *Ping!* Respond!

For those of us who remember that not-too-distant time, we all once had a telephone that was plugged into a wall outlet. The advent of wireless handsets released us from the twenty-foot cord that most of us had connected to our handset. We were all excited about it, and coupled with an answering machine that allowed us to record missed calls and screen calls, life was great. We were in control. We could return calls when we had time to do so. We didn't always feel compelled to answer the phone. And when we did, we had time to leisurely enjoy a glass of wine in the evenings while talking to a friend when moments without the television were cherished, quiet times for focusing on our friends and families during a phone conversation that could last for a significant amount of time—time enough to really exchange ideas at a time of our own choosing.

And then came the advent of the desktop computer and with it, email. At first, in its infancy, email was a novel way to stay in touch with distant friends and family without the cost of long-distance phone calls. It was fun. We would sit down and begin composing—yes, composing—an email to stay in touch, relay some news, share a moment. It didn't replace the cherished phone call, but it did provide another form of connection and familiarity with those we knew and loved. And it was not done by frantically typing with cryptic abbreviations and emojis.

And then, email entered the workplace. It was a defining moment in the existence of humanity; life would never be the same. I remember getting those phone calls that we all received in the beginning of the email introduction at the workplace, which transformed our focus at work when the boss called and exclaimed in various levels of, let's call it urgency, "Did you see my email!" Work moved from performing a task to watching for the boss's emails. Suddenly, we were like Pavlov's dogs, responding to the *ping* of an email message. But there was no reward from Pavlov. There was only anticipatory anxiety as we cautiously opened the email, wondering what our days would be like once the contents were read.

And try as we may to ignore them, or at least hold off from opening them until after lunch, they just sit there like a pulsating pain, filling our minds with anxieties and worries over their contents.

We learned, too, that our bosses, if they read our responses at all, don't really read beyond the first couple of sentences. Water-cooler conversations began to discuss how best to respond to the bosses' emails. "Do they read beyond the first sentence? The second sentence?" And our own ponderings: *Did they understand my email? Did they speed-read through it to get to the next email? Did they read it at all?* Life became consumed with how to respond to emails. And how our bosses would respond to ours.

But most of us have experienced responding to our boss's email, only then to have them reprimand us for not responding, as they never read it since it was way down on their list of unopened emails. Slowly, the one-on-one weekly update and strategy meetings with our bosses began to disappear from our calendars and were replaced by a constant stream of email messages. With them went the art of discussion. We had moved into the time of "Just answers. Now!"

I'll save for another time the discussion on emails from bosses who never used spell-check, or angrily typed in all capitals, all lowercase, without punctuation, or in one run-on sentence, or those emails sent to us at 3:00 a.m. (which were usually ominous unless your boss was sending them from Europe).

And then came the work email spillage into our personal life. Remember those times prior to email when the only anxiety we felt through electronic correspondence at home was when the phone rang at an odd hour? The message was usually truly urgent, requiring our attention because a family member or friend was ill. Seldom, if ever, did work at odd hours invade our homelife.

But the work emails did invade our home desktops and then laptops. The boundaries between work life and homelife started to dissolve. We became captive to our work email address—checking emails before bedtime became an obsession, resulting in lost sleep. Not checking our emails before bed also resulted in lost sleep while we worried about what we may be held accountable for the next day that we didn't read about the night prior.

Our time was still our own before the advent of email. We were called upon to respond only when we were really needed for family or friends. Life was truly simpler then.

Less anxiety for most of us. Time to think in the evenings and time to relax our bodies and our minds, time to focus. Time to spend with our family and friends over a meal or during an evening of back-porch conversation. We didn't live with the necessity of needing to check emails. We didn't live with the email anxiety of what-ifs. Emails didn't exist and certainly were inconceivable before they were conceived. And life was okay prior to email.

So then came cell phones. I remember succumbing to buying one after peer pressure got the best of me. Did I need it? At the time, no. Did I want it? Not really, but I felt I needed to have one because everyone said I needed to have one. Suddenly I had two phone numbers. Mom and Dad still called me on my home phone, and if I wasn't home, they left a message on my answering machine. I returned their calls at my leisure, when we could have a real conversation. Who did call my cell phone was my boss, who now had yet another way to invade my life outside of work with yet another form of anxiety, which would surface as my cell rang and I saw my boss's name on the cell phone's screen. *Should I pick up? Should I let it go into voicemail? What will be the repercussions of either decision?*

But the cell phone began to replace my home phone as my means of electronic communications. It came with a new anxiety: the battery charge on my phone required constant vigilance. We lost some of our privacy with email and certainly work emails, but the cell phone took over whatever remained of my personal time. And it invaded evening dinner hours and reading hours, and watching-the-nightly-news hours and Saturdays and Sundays.

Friends still respected a casual get-together for dinner; they did it by "silencing" their phones. The phones could still vibrate with an incoming call, however, as they sat there on the table, an ever-present little agitator eager for attention, and when not receiving enough of it, demanding it with an interrupting vibration of what could be an utmost urgent need. "Oh, it's my dry cleaner. Can you hold that thought about your mother's hospitalization while I take this call? It is important."

Once, during a gathering of friends over dinner at a local restaurant, my friend Della told another of our friends at the table to "Turn off your phone and put it away." The look of disbelief from our friend brought silence to the conversation at hand. After that, our friend seemed to have a look of anxiety as dinner progressed. I felt as if our phone-dependent friend had one hand ready at all times to grab the phone if from its silence, it suddenly sprang to life on its own with a series of vibrations.

And we all have tried to turn off our phones for periods of peacefulness. I don't need to discuss this, as the anxiety of our cell phones not being on overtakes all of us as we find ourselves succumbing to clicking On once again. Personal peace seems now to only be achieved if the cell phone is on, a peace we allow to be interrupted by the *ping* of a phone. And silence is never truly silence anymore, as we permit our cell phones to interrupt it at any moment.

And now, texting. Email has been reduced to what seems to be a series of dots and dashes, a form of Morse code that we are all expected to understand. Words can now be a string of abbreviated letters, many of which I often need to ponder for a while before I have any clue as to what they were meant to represent. Sometimes I just give up trying to interpret them. Gone are full sentences. Gone are the use of actual words. We now have texting in which everything is urgent, and every urgency can be answered with an emoji or a series of cryptic abbreviations.

With many words now expressed with emojis, for me this simply means why type the eight letters and one space to say thank you when a smiley face can do the same? And I hate autocorrect, which usually finds great pleasure in taking my sentences and interpreting them in their own way after I hit Send, probably thinking it is being funny or doing it as an act of revenge against me. And I find the act of typing a text to be a challenge in itself. The only people who don't feel frustration with typing a text may be six-year-olds whose fingers are still small enough to accurately hit all the keys.

But cell phones and texting are now a way of life, and they aren't going away.

So I use them as I continue to use sticky notes.

Do I consider them necessities? No. Will I continue to use emojis? Probably. Will I use cryptic abbreviations for words when texting? No. Will I continue to be frustrated with autocorrect or have difficulty typing on a keyboard designed for the fingers of a child? Yes. Will I continue to pay exorbitant prices for cell phones and all the accoutrements and mysterious charges that come with them, knowing that at one time in my life they didn't exist and all was well with me, with my family, and with the world around me? Yes.

Now, I can't imagine not having the immediate ability to snap a photo of some moment in time that three weeks later I will have completely forgotten and will wonder why I took the photo.

But will I cherish those long phone calls with family and friends now done on my cell phone? Absolutely.

I recently had a two-hour conversation with my friend Rita while sitting in my hotel room in another country. This could not have happened without my cell and the international dialing that comes with it. It was followed by a few texts between us, follow-ups from our conversation. For this, I am grateful for my cell phone and the technology that allows me to share this time with Rita. And photos.

But if cell phones and texting and emails went away, what would happen to all the anxiety that now consumes my life because of them? Yes, what would I do with it if I had to once again use a paper clip to fasten a note to a document I read, instead of a sticky note, or to spend one-half hour with a friend on the phone with a twenty-foot cord attached to its handset, nursing a glass of wine and having a conversation *without being interrupted by an incoming smiley face*?

Yes, what would I do?

Angels and Children

My cousin Linda passed in 2017. At the time, her daughter Sarah was soon to give birth to Linda's first grandchild, a little girl. Linda was very excited to be a grandmother, but her time had come, and Linda moved on to her next life. Sarah named her new daughter Larimar. Larimar is the name of a gemstone, the blue hues of which suggest the color of the Caribbean Sea. This stone is said to possess ancient metaphysical properties that enlighten and heal in physical, emotional, mental, and spiritual ways.

As Larimar grew, she became the spitting image of Linda, complete with Linda's exuberant personality.

Daughter number two, Lydia, then came along for Sarah and her husband. As of this writing, Lydia is now four years old. While Sarah was out on an errand recently, four-year-old Lydia, from the car's back seat, asked Sarah how Linda died.

Sarah asked Lydia, "Why do you want to know?"

Lydia replied, "Because I see Grandma Linda in the sky every morning when I look out the window."

I believe in angels.

I was once told that babies and young children can see angels, and as they mature, these little ones become more aware of their earthly surroundings and begin to lose their ability to consciously see angels. But the angels are still there.

My Catholic education taught me that we have guardian angels with us from birth onward. They are there, perhaps assigned to us, perhaps volunteering to be with us, to guide and protect us. They are our voice of reason and consciousness, supporting our souls, which I was taught are images of good. When our minds tend to stray away from good, our guardian angels tap us on our shoulders to remind us to lean back into the goodness of our souls. I think we all feel this in some way at times. I am grateful for my guardian angel's presence in my life. And I feel that my guardian angel has tapped me on my shoulder many times to get me to lean back into my soul, back into good, and perhaps at times has smacked me "upside my head" to more strongly remind me to lean back.

Maybe Linda volunteered to be Lydia's guardian angel.

Maybe Lydia's vision of Linda in the sky was Linda's way of saying, "Hey! I'm here for you." Linda often started her opening sentences with "Hey!"

It fascinates me, now that I am older and have time to think about things, things such as how babies tend to stare into space yet seem to be looking at something. Their gaze is often fixed. Yes, they seem to be looking at their mom or dad, sister or brother, but, too, they seem at times to be looking beyond or through them to something off in space.

Perhaps, this is when they are looking at angels or making their first acquaintance with their personal guardian angel.

The gentle, somewhat-gauzy image of an angel, the calming peaceful face looking down with a warming smile, robe flowing in ethereal breezes, and, of course, magnificent wings slowly moving would certainly fix a baby's stare. Perhaps there is recognition by the infant's soul that transmits to their early mind the knowledge of their guardian angel. Perhaps they already met just prior to when the baby's earthly life began, and now the guardian angel is saying, "I'm here for you." There is something about the stare of a baby that seems to echo this for me.

As Catholic children, we are taught early in our lives a prayer to our guardian angels.

Angel of God, my guardian dear,

To whom God's love entrusts me here.

Ever this day, be at my side,

To light and guard,

To rule and guide.

Amen.

It is an amazing moment to hear a room of young children reciting this prayer. There is something about their innocence that seems to connect them closer to the meaning of these words and to the presence of their angels. As Catholic kids, it is one of our earliest prayers memorized and recited with hands folded in prayer and heads slightly bowed in a position of humbleness.

Often, after the conclusion of Mass at my church and prior to exiting, the priests will offer a prayer that the congregation recites in unison. Father Enzo often offers the Hail Mary for the support of Mary, a prayer invoking the motherly guidance and intervention of Mary, the Mother of Jesus. Recently, Father John started his post-Mass prayer with "Angel of God…" It is not a prayer we often hear at Mass, but…

…the entire congregation, mostly adults, joined Father John in this prayer to their guardian angels. I was amazed. Amazed at what was happening around me—the entire congregation remembered the prayer to their guardian angels from the innocence of their childhoods and were now there, in church, reciting it together as they probably once did when they learned it in their elementary catechism classes.

Another prayer taught to us very early in life, still present, still top of mind, still at the tips of the tongues of everyone present. Still with deep meaning. They all remembered this prayer as clearly as they do the Lord's Prayer and the Hail Mary.

I too recited this prayer to my guardian angel at that Mass. And together, with a congregation of friends, associates, and strangers around me, we were all there, acknowledging the support and guidance, the protection and love of our guardian angels, an acknowledgment through a prayer we learned very early in childhood, our young hands folded in prayer and heads slightly bowed.

Grandma Olson II

When I was old enough to ride my two-wheeled gold-and-white spider bike with the banana seat and monkey handlebars on the street, Grandma Olson often called Mom and said, "Send Rodney up. I just made bread." I dropped whatever I was doing at that moment, as a warm roll with butter was awaiting me on my arrival.

On the way, I sometimes stopped to pick a bouquet of bright-orange tiger lilies that grew wild across from the home of my friend Wendy Stewart, which sat along the road leading to Marshall Heights. Grandma was always gracious in receiving them, putting them in a vase, and placing them in her dining room as I watched. She always made a fuss over my simple gift of wildflowers that grew along the road.

Grandma Olson lived on Marshall Heights, a subdivision of my childhood hometown of Black Lick, Pennsylvania. We lived *in* Edgemont; Grandma lived *on* Marshall Heights. Her home was really situated on a hill; the road leading up to it was every driver's nightmare when it snowed.

Grandma's neighbor to the right was Sally Palmer. Everyone called her by both names. Mrs. Palmer, a retired schoolteacher, lived in a white Craftsman-style home that sat above Grandma's home. Years before, someone had built a stone wall that supported and separated Mrs. Palmer's raised yard from Grandma's yard. Stone steps connected the yards. As a kid, I was always afraid of snakes that could possibly be living in the stone wall.

Across the street lived Mrs. Bennett. She was Grandma's best friend. She was also the grandmother of Joni, my childhood friend from Edgemont. Mrs. Bennett lived in a two story, brown-shingled home with white trim. Down the street lived Tatter Mandredi. I don't remember Tatter's real name, but I do remember the Mandredi family was friends with Grandma and Pap Bernini. Tatter, too, was a friend of Dad's.

When I was very young, Grandma had an upper garden and a lower garden. The upper garden was quite large and sat away from the home, adjacent to the wooded area of Mrs. Palmer's yard. The lower garden was closer to Grandma's kitchen door. I suspect that the upper garden was Grandma's "canning garden" and was used to raise bulk vegetables for her fall canning. The lower garden may have been her "kitchen garden," the place to run for a tomato or two and some fresh-cut lettuce when making a salad for dinner. Grandma's kitchen garden had a large, beautiful purple lilac bush next to it. When in bloom, the scent of lilac wafted into her kitchen and over us. The scent of lilac now brings this memory back to me every time. I love the scent of lilacs.

The gardens were separated by Grandma's two very bushy green-apple trees. The trees were quite bountiful when in season. Grandma made her apple pies from the slightly sour apples they produced. The dough for her crusts was always handmade using lard and, later, vegetable shortening. No matter what she used, the crusts flaked away and turned to butter in your mouth. Her apple pies have no adjectives to describe their delectability. The same for her bread and rolls. I know I was lucky to have her as my grandma. So was my brother and our twenty-two first cousins.

When in season, my cousin Linda and I could often be found plodding around those apple trees to find just the right apples and pick them from the low-hanging branches. After rubbing them against our shirts to shine them, we crunched into them, which resulted in their juices running down our chins. When Grandma watched us for our mothers during the summers, the apple trees were definitely on our agenda. Grandma would yell out to us from her kitchen door, "Hey, you two! Don't eat too many of those! You'll get a tummy ache." We listened. For the most part, we were good kids when together. For the most part. Linda's mother may disagree.

Grandma's clothesline sat next to the apple trees running alongside the upper garden. She kept a high chair in her kitchen for her growing lot of grandkids. I remember a time when she was babysitting my brother and me and had placed Bobby in the high chair while she was vacuuming. It was a washing and housecleaning day for Grandma. She already had her sheets on the clothesline and was busy running her upright Hoover vacuum in the living room when she looked out her dining room windows and saw that the clothesline holding her sparkling-white sheets had drooped a little from their weight. The sheets were about to touch the ground.

Grandma beckoned to me to run out the kitchen door and prop up the clothesline for her. Of course, I would! Grandma had several clothesline poles, some made of wood and a few newer ones made of aluminum. They always were lying parallel to each other under her clothesline, rain or shine. I remember that I could maneuver the wooden ones easier than the metal ones. So off I went.

After sizing up the operation, seven-year-old me reached down to grab one of the wooden clothesline poles. It moved. It wasn't a clothesline pole. It was a very large black snake. I jumped back with a shout.

Mrs. Bennett heard my hysterical screaming from across the road, almost two houses away. She came bounding out her front door, crossed the street, ran through Grandma's yard, and grabbed me. I could barely explain what just happened. Mrs. Bennett took my hand and led me toward Grandma's kitchen door, explaining to me that black snakes can't hurt me.

For me, at that moment, I didn't care. A snake was a snake. I always feared that they could live in that stone wall separating Grandma's yard from Mrs. Palmer's yard. I was justified in my fear and now terrified with fright.

Mrs. Bennett took me into Grandma's house. Grandma was busy with her vacuuming and didn't hear my screaming. My little brother was calm, playing in his high chair. Mrs. Bennett explained the situation to Grandma. Grandma hugged me. All was suddenly right with the world again. Well, all was right except that I wasn't going out again to prop up the clothesline. Maybe never again.

I loved Grandma Olson, and I loved spending time with her. I think most kids may feel that way about their grandmothers. She was often baking pies or bread or rolls; the result, her home was always a sensory delight. Sometimes she made waffles and served them with her wonderful floured, fried chicken and gravy, or she made her buckwheat pancakes and late in the day called Mom to say, "Why don't you and Billy bring the boys up for dinner? I am making buckwheat pancakes with simple syrup tonight."

Grandma's stewed tomatoes were legendary, as was her "Hamburg gravy," a gravy made with lots of ground beef and served over mashed potatoes. She taught Mom to make many of her recipes, which Mom learned to perfect. And I loved her creamed beets. Grandma's meals were always simple, made with real ingredients by her loving hands, and incredibly tasty. On occasion, she gave us a jar or two of her homemade apple butter. I find it amazing how, after all these years, my sense of taste and smell still hold on to those precious tastes and aromas.

Dad often told the story of watching his mother and her sisters making apple butter outdoors on a chilly autumn day in a copper kettle heated underneath by a wood fire. Grandma's days of kettle-made apple butter had passed by the time I came around. One day, Dad showed up at our house with a large copper kettle and its iron frame. I remember he vigorously cleaned it with vinegar to brighten the copper interior. Clearly, Grandma's apple butter and the making of it was a very special memory for him.

We never used the large kettle for making apple butter, but Dad did pull it out of the garage and place it in the alley, centered between our neighbors' homes, for our Independence Day and Memorial Day neighborhood picnics. A wood fire underneath was used to boil water in which white pillowcases filled with shucked, fresh-picked corn on the cob from the local farms was cooked for the picnics. When the corn was done and the pillowcases containing it were pulled from the kettle, suddenly out of nowhere would appear a grouping of us neighborhood kids watching every move as the corn was spilled from the pillowcases onto a plastic tablecloth. I don't need to explain what happened next.

***

Dad came home on another day with three large clay pots. They were simply known as crocks to us back then; now they are collector's items. Dad explained that he was going to use them to make root beer as his mother did when he was a kid. So after a meticulous scrubbing, Dad took me shopping for the ingredients to make root beer. He bottled three to four dozen bottles about every six weeks. I was always present, as was my brother, for the Saturday-afternoon event in our basement. I assisted in the filling of the "pop" bottles Dad had saved for his homemade root beer. We even had a bottle capper, which was a challenge for me to use, but I did often try, Dad's hand over mine, to apply enough pressure to the lever during the capping process.

The root-beer slurry required yeast for the fermentation process. It came in cake form, wrapped in red, waxy paper. I loved the smell of it as it was being unwrapped. Dad let me taste the pure yeast, a taste I quickly learned to love. But Dad also warned me that I could only taste it and not eat it, as the yeast cells would grow in my tummy. Another potential issue for my tummy…

Dad, with Mom's permission, laid the bottles of newly made root beer on their sides on the steps leading to our attic. It was there they would ferment, creating the fizz that root beer should have. This continued for several years until, one summer, the attic steps became too hot from the heat trapped in the attic, and the fermentation process went wild. Caps started popping off when we were away from home one day. When we returned, root beer was flowing down the attic steps and seeping through to the ceiling of the stairway below them, leading to our basement family room. The root-beer making ended soon after.

***

Mom and Dad often bought their beef and pork directly from a local farm. They did the same for our milk. Saturdays usually meant a drive to Cornell's dairy farm with our eight one-half-gallon glass milk jugs in their wire carriers, each of which held four bottles. When filled, my skinny little self needed to use two hands to carry one of these carriers to the car. Cornell's had a small storefront for their milk business. Behind the counter was a large glass window through which we could watch some of the milk processing taking place. If we went early enough, sometimes we could watch the cows being milked.

My job, other than helping by struggling to carry the milk to the car, was to hold my little brother's hand while in the shop. I did this in most places we went if Mom or Dad weren't holding his hand. It's the assigned job of older siblings. I liked my little brother, so it was never an issue for me unless his hands were sticky from a previously dripping ice-cream cone. But I must also admit that, being who my brother and I are, we didn't often have the dreaded sticky hands from dripping ice-cream cones.

The milk was pasteurized and homogenized, but sometimes a newly opened bottle had a little cream on top of the milk. Going to farms was a natural for us; if it wasn't for beef or pork, it was for apples in the autumn or the weekly milk run. Mom loved to watch cows grazing in fields, so Dad sometimes picked up Grandma and took all of us on Sunday drives through the countryside, pulling the car to the side of a road next to a field of cows for Mom to watch them graze. She was always thrilled when one or two would mosey over to the fence separating us from them, to check us out. Cows have beautiful eyes.

***

Sometimes Dad went alone on the farm errands if we were sick or busy with school functions. Once, he came home with three beheaded chickens, feathers still intact. He told Mom that he was hungry for fresh chicken, the kind Grandma made when he was a kid at home. Dad went on to say that fresh chicken tasted nothing like store-bought chicken. Pap, my mother's father, was a part-time butcher when she was a young girl, so she fully understood.

Mom asked where the chickens were. Dad said they were in a bag in the garage. Mom said they were going to remain there because she didn't want them in the house, and she wasn't going to touch them. Dad thought Mom knew how to clean a freshly killed chicken. She didn't.

As I stood in the kitchen watching this exchange between them about the three headless chickens in our garage (my curiosity was under control that day and did not lead me to look at them), Mom and Dad both realized that neither of them knew what to do with the chickens in a bag in our garage. So Mom did what she always did when a food-related crisis arose, she called her oldest brother's wife, my aunt Dolly.

Aunt Dolly told her she would take them, as she knew how to pluck and clean a chicken. Uncle Pete soon arrived in his red-and-white Ford pickup truck, with the raised bed cover that he and Uncle Mario made, and took the chickens away. I know nothing more about them.

***

But my memories digressed…

Dad had taught me to put together model cars, the molded-plastic models that required airplane glue for the assembly. I was hooked…on the model cars, not the glue. I believe airplane glue is now off the market for projects like these for kids. I didn't like the smell of it, but it did what I needed it to do, so I dealt with the smell. I was always careful, though, as once dripped, the glue was permanently there, and once on my fingers, it took days to wear off. In our family room, Dad set up a special desk at which I could put my models together with no fear of an impending airplane-glue mess.

One summer, Grandma did a lot of babysitting for my brother and me. That summer often found me in Grandma's living room, where she would spread newspaper on her coffee table so I could assemble and glue my model cars. I guess after raising ten children and now having me, sixth oldest in a line of grandkids, she had a level of tolerance for impending kid disasters that only comes with age and experience and being a grandmother.

So there I would sit while she cleaned or cooked, and while my brother busied himself with his toy cars on the floor next to me. At a certain morning hour, all would stop when Grandma called her youngest sister, Georgia, whom we all called Aunt Georgie. I was told as a young kid that Aunt Georgie's husband, Great-Uncle Jock, had served in World War I in his youth. It was there he was "gassed," as so many young men were who fought in that war. I had no idea then what this meant, other than Uncle Jock had some trouble breathing. I discovered later in life, during my independent studies on World War I, what this unconscionable act of war meant to those who were "gassed."

Grandma's black dial phone sat on a pedestal in her dining room. She had one of her blue-damask upholstered dining room chairs sitting next to it. There she sat, spending what seemed to always be forever on the phone with Aunt Georgie. This was only interrupted when it was time for lunch for my brother and me.

Lunch was always served to us at her kitchen table. I had free rein to search the contents of her refrigerator for food I may like. As you may recall, I was a problem eater, and Grandma (I think) graciously understood my nuances. Once, I found buttermilk in her refrigerator. She told me she had liked it since she was a young girl and offered a juice glass of it to me. I never came near it again.

Lunch had to be completed and dishes washed by the time *The Guiding Light* came on the television. All stopped, including any noise from either of her two grandsons. I continued with my model cars during this time, my brother with his toy cars. We didn't complain. We simply respected the requirement of ultimate quiet for Grandma's ultimate focus on the television.

When staying with Grandma, I remember, too, that she often had buttered toast and a cup of coffee for breakfast or lunch. She would dip her toast in the coffee while eating it. She once offered the same to me at her home. I could understand why she liked it.

Grandma lived in a green Craftsman-style home. It had a long interior stairway with, partway up, a landing that turned right and continued a few steps more to the second floor. The second floor had four bedrooms, a room which was a former sleeping porch, and a bathroom containing a large claw-foot tub. I never liked the tub. For a young boy, it was hard to get into and out of. And it was deep. I always felt small in it. My dad's youngest brother was still living at home and dating at this time, so the bathroom usually had the telltale scent of pomade and Old Spice. Grandma wore rosewater perfume, which permeated the second level of her home, at times, from her bedroom.

Cousin Linda and I, when Grandma babysat us together, had a grand time on that second level. We explored every room, used the mattress on the bed in the back bedroom as a trampoline, and checked out various closets. The closet in the sunroom was the best to explore. It held the Christmas decorations. Periodically, we heard Grandma yell up the steps, "Hey! What are you two doing up there?" If it was about the trampoline, we were quick to remake the bed as best we could.

While Grandma often had my family for dinner, Mom would just as often have Grandma over for dinner. The menu varied between a roast with potatoes to something Italian. Grandma like to have a cup of coffee with her dinner, so Mom always made sure a fresh pot of coffee was brewing before Grandma arrived. Grandma used milk in her coffee. She always sat at the head of the table; Dad was opposite her, at the other end. My job, when old enough, was to take Grandma's coffee to her just before the meal began. Mom always ensured it was served in a cup and saucer accompanied by a creamer of milk.

When I was very young, Grandma hosted her ten children and their spouses for Sunday or holiday dinners when they were all visiting at the same time from their different homes, now in different states. Yes, twenty adults and their gaggle of kids. And yes, Grandma did all the cooking! The adults were all dressed in their Sunday best and sat in Grandma's formal dining room with its imposing sideboard and large china cabinet with intricate woodwork on the glass doors holding the glass in place. The china cabinet held her china with an autumnal pattern on it. It also held her collection of porcelain teacups. Grandma collected these during her travels; a large share of them were from her time in Europe when visiting her daughter Joyce; Aunt Joyce's husband was stationed in Germany during his army career. What none of us knew at that time was that one teacup each was to be given to her grandchildren upon her passing.

The dinners were always formal but a lot of fun. Grandma knew how to set a beautiful table, which was always lighted by the large 1920s-era chandelier of pinkish-beige milk glass that hung above it. We kids, the boys always dressed in suits and the girls in flouncy little church dresses, sat at a large child-sized table in the adjacent living room. Dinners started with a juice glass of cold tomato juice, Grandma's signature appetizer from earlier days. I remember Aunt Illa Roi or Aunt Ruth always coming in during dinner to check on us. We were a well-behaved group of kids. But then, I don't think we would have *even dared* to be anything but well-behaved on these occasions at Grandma's.

There wasn't a holiday that Grandma didn't come to our home after church to spend an hour or so with us before moving on to the home of her youngest daughter, Helen, to see Cousin Linda and her brothers, Kevin and Robb. Grandma always had envelopes for my brother and me and handed them to us with a smile, a hug, and a kiss. Sometimes she stayed at our home for holiday lunch.

As life moved on and I started to drive, Dad often asked me if I had visited "Mom" recently. When I left for college, this was always a question that better be answered with a yes. I certainly didn't mind. I remember going to see Grandma in my tuxedo before proms to show the tux to her. I did the same in my cap and gown when graduating from high school. I had hoped she could attend my graduation ceremony, but her health was beginning to slide.

Grandma sat for a formal photograph when I was in my early teens. She had several wallet-sized photos of it laminated. One Sunday, she came to our home and wanted to see me alone. She handed me an envelope. In it was one of her laminated photos and a letter to me. In the letter, she told me that the photo was for my wallet, but if it didn't fit because of all the photos of my girlfriends, it was okay. She told me that she loved me, as she loved all her grandchildren. There was more in the letter. I still have it and her photo. Both sit in my album of special memories. The rest of the letter will remain between Grandma and me. That's the way I want it.

***

I received a call from my dad one night while I was in graduate school at the University of Pittsburgh. He told me to immediately drive over to Saint Margaret's Hospital in Aspinwall; I needed to see my grandmother. Now. It was December, and I was in the middle of finals. But I didn't waste any time. When I arrived, my dad's seven sisters and only living brother were outside of Grandma's room. Aunt Joanne was in with Grandma, but soon came out.

Aunt Joyce told me to go in. I did. There was my grandma, in a hospital bed, propped up. She looked sideways at me.

Her big blue eyes smiled first; then she smiled and said, "Rodney." I walked over to kiss her. She said, "You came to see your grandma."

I don't remember the rest of the exchange we had. It was a short conversation. She kept looking at me. Perhaps her memories were flooding back to model cars and tiger lilies and the clothesline-pole incident. Perhaps she was just taking me in. I was taking her in.

I didn't want to leave, but was not permitted to stay.

I kissed her again as I left and told her I loved her.

Aunt Joanne was holding my grandma's hand as she passed.

***

Grandma Olson was the only grandparent I ever knew. My mom's parents and Granddad Olson passed before I was born. My older Bernini cousins have equally wonderful stories of their times with Grandma Bernini and Pap. Granddad Olson passed when the oldest of my Olson cousins were very young.

Grandma's gentle and genteel self were always present in my life; her wonderful food and kindly, patient manner are very much a part of my lasting memories of her. Although she has now passed on to her next life, she is still with me, and I hope her presence will always be there.

When my dad asked me if there was anything of Grandma's that I would like to have, in addition to the teacup, I was quick to answer. I wanted the pedestal on which her black dial telephone sat. For me, it held the memories of Grandma talking to Aunt Georgie while my little brother and I played within sight of her when she babysat us. Unfortunately, the pedestal was lost in the flurry of inheritance activities. But I can still see it…and Grandma sitting next to it, chatting away.

The memories of people we once knew are sometimes too precious to fade into the recesses of our minds. These memories pop up at unexpected moments when we hear something, or see a jar of apple butter or a carton of buttermilk in the grocery store, or while watching a television show. And sometimes our minds just drift off on their own and then come back to reality; at that moment, we realize that we missed the last ten minutes of the nightly news while our minds were in another place, another time.

The memories tend to be disjointed, though; the threads that once wove them together are not as apparent any longer. A kitchen scene here, a wildflower moment there, a younger brother playing next to you—all lead to a non sequitur series of thoughts that flash back at the same time while you are in the kitchen preparing a meal, in the shower, or driving on an endless stretch of highway.

They live on, through us, because we want them to live on. And perhaps, we need them to live on.

Hello

I am back in Mexico City. I continue to be constantly amazed at the warm greetings most people give to one another here. I have often written about people in the office in which I work, the "*holas*" and "*cómo estás*" in the elevators in the morning, greetings from people whom I am often seeing for the first time, but being made to feel as if we were old acquaintances. Strangers, yet exchanges as if we were not. Friendly smiles when eyes meet.

Colleagues at the office all greet each other and me in an even more cordial manner: women offer air-kisses as cheeks meet while embracing; men offer firm handshakes, then a shoulder bump while embracing, followed by a second firm handshake. Eyes always meet.

I have learned to expect this. And I have learned to return it without an awkward feeling of being too personal. I now feel comfortable with these exchanges and enjoy returning this warm greeting, as well as initiating them on my own.

In my office life prior to Mexico and in Madrid where I worked, similar greetings were given, but people didn't touch, other than a handshake only when absolutely required. Elevators tended to be places where heads were down, often scanning cell phones wildly and certainly avoiding eye contact. People tended not to want to speak. Office exchanges in the morning were usually absent as people scurried to their desks, coffee or tea in hand, in a rush to what seemed to be avoidance of all interactions with fellow human beings.

This still continues.

I, too, have been guilty of this.

And I now find this sad.

There seems to be something joyous about these greetings in Mexico City that are offered freely by just about everyone. Smiles are exchanged; eye contact is made. These exchanges tend not to be hollow, perfunctory moments; they are meaningful. Whether they go deeper than the surface doesn't seem to matter, as the manner in which the greeting is usually given touches something inside. A genuineness seems to be present that reaches the soul.

I recently heard a sermon by a minister in New York City; he stated that there is a need for "souls to catch up with our bodies." His phrase made me stop to grab a pencil and notepad and quickly jot this concept down. His sermon was centered on the rapid way in which too many of us live our lives on "fast-forward." We "gotta get 'it' done" to move on to the next "gotta get 'it' done." Rush to the next appointment; scroll for your life through text messages, emails, and social media messages. Register a "like" because... well, because there is no time to ponder what you are liking because something else needs to be skimmed for its surface meaning before moving on to the next.

We seem to have evolved into beings who don't have time to allow things to penetrate...and, perhaps, meaningful exchanges between other human beings top this list.

Maybe this is just a New York City thing. But I don't think so. My parents could sit for hours in the evenings on their back porch with neighbors or relatives. People talked, reflected, shared concerns face-to-face. They didn't learn about someone's needs or concerns in the sterile environment of a text or email, where emotions that can only be fully understood by facial expressions are absent.

I, too, once could sit for hours in college during study breaks to converse with my friends while sitting on each other's beds or at each other's desks, or moving between both. Sometimes music was playing, but the conversations took place over it. We were allowed the time to express concerns, vent, laugh, recall events that were happy or sad, or just funny. If we liked something while talking, it was a verbal "like." With a human smile. We had an exchange of conversation, just as our parents had on their back porches or at their kitchen tables or in their living rooms when relatives "stopped in." Or when neighbors "came over."

These times just occurred. They weren't scheduled.

They weren't interrupted by a phone pinging with a message or ringing with a call.

And we looked at each other.

Uncle Pete

My sophomore year at Saint Vincent College was a big move-in event for me. I was now living in an upperclassmen dorm with a room that was much larger than the freshman rooms of Aurelius Hall. My dorm was named Bonaventure. That, in itself, brought a sense of connection for me, reminding me often of the church that I—and most of my mother's family—grew up with: Saint Bonaventure Church in Palmertown.

I had been in contact with my roommate; I was bringing a dorm-sized refrigerator. This was easy for me, as I could use my discount to buy it from Montgomery Ward in Indiana, Pennsylvania, where I worked in the catalog stockroom during the summers for money for college.

My move included the refrigerator as well as my clothes, bedding and shower linens, and books. Mom asked her oldest brother, my uncle Pete, to help with my move when the time came. Of course, he would; he would do anything for his youngest sister.

Uncle Pete loaded the back of his red-and-white Ford truck with my suitcases and boxes of stuff. Off we went to Latrobe, Pennsylvania, eventually turning right onto Frasier Purchase Road, another right into the Saint Vincent campus, and finally up the hill to Bonaventure Hall, which we called Bonnie.

Uncle Pete helped to unload the truck. My uncle Pete. My surrogate grandfather. Both my grandfathers had moved on to their next life prior to my birth. But Uncle Pete, somewhere in my later childhood, seemed to start to fill that position for me. I sat with him at times as a kid during Mass at Saint Bonaventure. He was there with me sophomore year, and I was so thankful and so proud for him to be there. Together, he, Dad, and I made many trips back and forth from the truck and up many steps to my room.

I had a new roommate my junior year at Saint Vincent and was again in touch with him before move-in day for the fall semester. He was to bring his stereo; I was to bring my dorm-sized refrigerator. And my uncle Pete was once again there my junior year, transporting my growing number of boxes and that refrigerator to my dorm room, now in Gerard Hall (a.k.a. Gerry). I honestly could not have imagined it any other way at the time. I was so grateful. Perhaps it was that year that I fully understood how the Bernini family was just that—family. They helped each other. No project was too big. Nothing seemed out of the question. Uncle Pete was sixty-seven years old that year.

Uncle Pete was born on April 5, 1909, to my grandmother Bernini and my pap. He was their firstborn of eight children. My mom was their last.

Uncle Pete was not there to move me into Gerard Hall my senior year. He passed on July 16, 1977, joining his infant son and my grandparents, his mama and pap, in heaven.

I felt the loss of Uncle Pete as Dad and I pulled into the parking lot in front of Gerard Hall the August of my senior year at Saint Vincent. Uncle Pete passed only a few weeks prior. The moment wasn't complete. My ride to campus in the front seat of my uncle's red pickup truck didn't happen that year; my college paraphernalia was not in the back of his truck. My surrogate grandfather wasn't there to help me move into my dorm, to crack a few jokes as we were working, to tease me as he always did, to shake my hand, to smile his big Bernini smile, and to wish me luck as he departed. That Bernini smile of assurance, comfort, and family was missing.

I still remember this moment as if it were yesterday. I still feel a tear of loss.

The Beautiful Paper-Flower Lady

During my first two years of working two consecutive weeks each month for my client in Mexico City, I often took a short walk to stretch my legs during the weekends that bridged my workweeks. Out of my own fears, I usually didn't travel too far, being in a strange city among strangers who seemingly sometimes recognized me as being from the United States. The Mexican people are very friendly, and total strangers will look at you with a pleasant hola while walking. But during some of my walks, when acknowledging strangers with a greeting in Spanish or just nodding, the response was often hello, which at times unnerved me. Did they know I was from the Unites States?

I tended to stay close to the hotel's neighborhood of Polanco during my walks. And I tended to travel the same routes. I enjoyed exploring the area. There was much to see and experience. I loved how most streets are tree-lined, providing ample shading over the sidewalks and counteracting the effects of climate change and pollution. I also loved the streets themselves, avenues lined with restaurants and homes, morphing into and out of business districts without ever losing the feel of a neighborhood. I was amazed at the number of Catholic churches and, during my rides to the office, at the number of people I saw entering them during weekday mornings. And during spring, the beautiful jacaranda trees with their dense foliage and lavender flowers that replace the usual greenery lining most streets. As the jacarandas shed their flowers' petals, the sidewalks become carpeted in lavender.

During one of my early walks one weekend, I decided to take a right out of the Intercontinental and walk along Calle Campos Eliseos, the street on which my hotel sits, rather than go straight and cross Campos Eliseos. To the left of my hotel is a JW Marriott, next to it is a W Hotel, and to the right of my hotel is a Hyatt. This section of Campos Eliseos seems to be the hotel district for Mexico City. I was curious about what was beyond the Hyatt when I made the decision to go right.

Crossing an entrance to the parking garage for the Intercontinental, I came upon a lady sitting on a blanket on the sidewalk. She had a shawl wrapped around her shoulders as she sat cross-legged with her back against a wall adjacent to the sidewalk. In front of her were several colorful plastic buckets of beautiful paper flowers. Each was intricately detailed, a work of art in its own right. The flowers were of various species, each clearly identifiable as a rose or a tulip, or some other beautiful creation of nature. I was intrigued.

The woman was in the process of creating another work of art as she looked up at me and smiled. I realized then that she was making the flowers to sell there on the street. She had a small bowl in which people passing by put donations, paying for a flower or two, which the woman graciously offered from her large array of stems. I took time to look over the flowers and then offered a donation. She motioned with her hand for me to choose a flower. I declined. She motioned again. I declined. She stood up and offered again. Neither of us clearly understood each other's language as we tried to communicate, but finally, after a smile and a *muchas-gracias*, she understood, and I departed.

On my next two-week visit, during my walk I decided to take that same right out of the Intercontinental and along Calle Campos Eliseos. There she was again, sitting on the ground with a different shawl wrapped around her shoulders. She seemed to recognize me and immediately held up one of her flower creations. I declined the offer. I would have taken it, but had no place to put it, and the delicate nature of it would not survive the trip home in my luggage. We exchanged smiles and conversation that neither of us fully understood. I do think she did understand my hand and eye motions signaling that I had to fly in a plane and the flowers would not survive. But, this time, during our eye-and-hand conversation, I felt something about her that registered a connection. I liked her for the person I could understand she was, without ever speaking her language.

I started to return to see her on each subsequent trip to Mexico City. Each time, she would quickly recognize me walking down the street and jump up to see me. At one point, she hugged me, and after that, we exchanged hugs with each greeting. Hugs in Mexico City are an acceptable form of greeting, no matter the person or the circumstance. Often, we exchanged conversations unknown to each other with laughs and smiles and hand motions. The conversations always ended with an offer of one of her beautiful, delicate creations. Once, she carefully selected three stems and thrust them into my hand as I was leaving. I had to take them. They certainly brought color to my hotel room of rich but sterile greys and browns.

***

We had just moved into our new ranch-style home on Elm Street in the Edgemont Section of my childhood hometown of Black Lick, Pennsylvania. The yard had yet to be landscaped; I think Dad may have been waiting on the landscape plans that his uncle John was developing. Great-Uncle John was a landscape professional and worked for Wesleyan University in West Virginia. His wife, my dad's aunt Betty, was an English-language professor at the same university.

After the foundation excavation, in our side yard there was a large dirt mound waiting to be leveled. It was a young boy's dream. My dream. During my developing friendship with Joey, who lived three houses over, I discovered that his collection of Tonka trucks complemented mine, and so we were often found on that dirt mound.

One day while playing on the dirt mound, Mom called me into the house and asked me if I wanted to go to the movies with Aunt Helen and my cousin Linda. They were going to see the newly released movie *Mary*

Poppins. I jumped on the offer. Mom told me to go to my bedroom and change into a white shirt, black pants, and my green sports jacket with the college emblem over the breast pocket. People once dressed for movies. Mom said to hurry, which I did.

I came out of my bedroom, passed Mom's eye test for my appearance, and ran out the door to meet Aunt Helen and Linda at the corner of our lot, where we would catch the Blairsville-to-Indiana bus to go see the movie in Indiana.

We boarded. I sat down next to Aunt Helen. Linda, who was five years old, then wedged between us. For some reason, I looked down at my hands and realized that I had forgotten to wash them after coming in from the dirt pile. They were filthy. I was mortified. Mom would be more than upset with me if she found out. So I put my hands in my pants pockets, and there they stayed until we were seated in the theater.

Aunt Helen ran to get popcorn for Linda and me. When she did, I took my hands out of my pockets and examined them. They were clean! Yes, clean! My hands had sweat so much on that summer day, while riding a bus that was not air-conditioned, that the dirt had rubbed off on the interior of my pants pockets. Saved! And more importantly, I could eat popcorn without Aunt Helen seeing my filthy hands.

As the movie progressed, I found myself totally engrossed in it. What kid wasn't during that day and age? The music was great, and the story line had me at "Supercalifragilistic-expialidocious." Then, Mary Poppins sang "Feed the Birds" to her wards, Michael and Jane Banks. As an eight-year-old, I was moved for the first time in my young memory by a song and felt a few tears forming. I watched the movie intently as the little old bird woman was feeding the birds while selling her crumbs for a tuppence a bag.

A few years ago, Linda and I were reminiscing on this shared movie experience, and I bought DVDs of *Mary Poppins* for both of us as a remembrance of that shared childhood event. When viewing the movie at that time in life, "Feed the Birds" brought me to tears once again.

Later, I checked out the lyrics. One line resonated deeply with me. It included a reference to "listen, listen." And with few words, the little old bird woman connected with the potential buyers of her crumbs. But as an adult, and many years later after seeing *Mary Poppins* with Aunt Helen and Linda, I now realize that these lyrics represent more than a sense performed by ears. It is a sense that also needs to be performed with the heart and, as referenced in the lyrics, demonstrating to someone that you care.

And maybe in this world we live in, in the cultures we share, this is part of the sense of listening that societies have forgotten to teach...and to do.

***

My interactions with this beautiful woman who made beautiful paper flowers on the sidewalk in Mexico City are over for now. I know nothing more about her, but wonder if her flower sales supported her children in some way, or an ill parent or husband, or perhaps she used the money to feed the birds. On my new engagement with my client in Mexico City, she was no longer on Calle Campos Eliseos, wrapped in a beautiful shawl, sitting on the sidewalk and making beautiful paper flowers. I wish she were there. I would love to see her again and experience her warm personality and welcoming smile and feel her gracious hug.

And once again communicate across cultures without understanding each other's language.

Perhaps it is in these moments, we "listen, listen," listen with our hearts.

Church

My church was filled last night—standing room only for Ash Wednesday. And it was Valentine's Day!

What also struck me was the number of young people—people in their twenties and thirties—there for Mass and to receive ashes, as traditionally administered in Roman Catholic churches on Ash Wednesday. "Ashes to ashes. Dust to dust" was repeated over and over again by Monsignor Sakano and Father Alex as they made the sign of the cross on the seemingly never-ending line of congregants, pew by pew, with people lining all the walls of the sanctuary and further extending into the narthex, all coming forward for this annual blessing.

The number of people, and specifically young people, was mentioned by several of the regulars who attend daily Mass with me. Paul, an older statesman in the church, was one. He said the evening reminded him of attending this same church, although now rebuilt, when he was a kid. The church was always overflowing for Ash Wednesday even then.

But again, this Ash Wednesday was Valentine's Day. Clearly there were many who felt it was important to receive ashes that evening before beginning their Valentine's Day celebrations. Well, that is, their *Saint* Valentine's Day celebrations. Their internal, very personal priority of receiving ashes first drove them through the doors of The Chapel to participate for about one hour in this annual entry into the Lenten season.

I often read how church attendance has been falling since the 1960s and of the surveys of the numbers of people who do not claim an affiliation to a church. Perhaps this is true, too, about temples and mosques, but I have never seen articles describing similar statistics for these religions. But, this night, I started to question the accuracy of these surveys. I was taught in my statistic courses in school that surveys and polls are only as good as the universe of people selected to participate in them. And I was taught how easy it is to manipulate the outcomes of surveys and polls by how the questions are posed and by not ensuring that the universe of participants is truly randomly selected.

What was that which drove so many people, and especially so many young people, to church before dinners and celebrations on this day dedicated to Cupid's arrow?

Whatever the driving force, it was reassuring to witness.

Sunflowers on First Avenue

During the pandemic and while in lockdown, I started walking two miles each morning before the start of my workday. Work did continue during this time, only now through Zoom and Teams, requiring that I be seated for hours. I started to feel I needed some movement for my body. After masking up, suiting up, and putting on my latex gloves (sometimes under my winter gloves), off I went, out the side door of my apartment building, taking a left on Thirty-Eighth Street and a right on Second Avenue, walking the vacant streets of Manhattan to Fifty-Seventh Street, then taking another right and walking to First Avenue, where I took another right onto vacant First Avenue, and then headed home past the vacated United Nations buildings. I could count the people on two hands that I encountered during these pandemic walks.

I eventually realized that I needed this morning walk. I found it a great time to reflect, prepare for the day's work, think through how to construct difficult emails, or prepare for difficult meetings, but most of all to clear my head and feel the outdoor air on my face. I am not sure today's culture of constant activity and stimulation respects the need for time for "clearing our heads." And how many times do we walk outside to just feel the air on our faces?

As I walked down the east side of First Avenue, I often cut across to the west side of First at Fortieth Street. I came to recognize a landmark that reminded me to cross, as I was usually deep in thought during my walks. The landmark was a large cement urn, about three feet high, filled with dirt. Clearly, it had been there for years. In it grew many varieties of struggling weeds, the seeds for which were probably dropped by the many birds flying overhead or the whipping winds off the nearby East River. And the urn was used as a receptacle for discarded plastic bottles and candy wrappers. Sad.

To the left of the urn is a large vacant lot that stretches from Thirty-Eight Street to Forty-First Street, from First Avenue to FDR Drive. The lot was once home to the Waterside (Electric) Generating Station, built in 1901 and later expanded by New York Con Edison, to finally be decommissioned in 1999 after conversion from coal to natural gas and a history of concerns regarding pollution affecting the United Nations. The ground has sunk over the years. The granite on which Manhattan sits is exposed in some areas. Rain collects in the gullies left behind by the backhoes and bulldozers that cleared the Con Ed buildings that once stood there.

The small lakes that form, I realized, are the notorious breeding grounds for the mosquitoes that can be found on apartment ceilings, pulsating with delight at the prospect of drinking from humans, during the warm summer months if windows are left open. The lot is usually overgrown with weeds, so it is anyone's guess what is residing under the weeds. Yes, this is quite a contrast from the

Manhattan of Rockefeller Center. I suspect the urn is all that remains of the entrance to the once-mighty Con Ed Generating Station. The history and passage of time locked in its existence must be daunting, as it sits alone on First Avenue.

One spring morning during my walk, I noticed that the lonely urn had been cleared of weeds and debris. A few days later, after a rain, I noticed some green stems popping through the cleared soil. A few days after that, I knew the green growth was the start of sunflowers. Some kind soul took pity on the lonely urn and decided to bring it to its former glory for the purpose it was designed.

I watched the growth and development of the little sunflowers with each day of my walk. My Western Pennsylvania upbringing in farm country was exploding with eagerness each day to see the new growth while waiting patiently for the first signs of a bud to appear.

***

I love living in Manhattan. I have loved it since first deplaning in Newark and taking a cab into Manhattan to begin my career and life there. I remember the cabdriver from the airport that evening had Joe Jackson's "Steppin' Out" playing on the radio, a song that always brings that night alive in me again. The culture and expansive knowledge that can be gained from the museums are perhaps two of the greatest opportunities here for me. The energy of the city has me addicted. But, from day one after moving into Manhattan from my garden apartment in Park Slope, Brooklyn, I have missed the soil.

This is not to say that I don't appreciate the greenery and dramatic landscapes of Central Park, or Saint Vartan's Park one block from my home. They are beautiful, but I cannot get down on my hands and knees, feel the soil, and plant a seed, or a tomato plant or a twig that will grow into a tree. Friends have asked if I could satisfy my desires by planting tomato plants in urns on my balcony. I could, but it isn't the same as having an expanse of land around me, being down on my knees with trowel in hand, and a box of starter tomato plants or packets of seeds nearby, feeling the sun on my back and the soil sifting through my fingers, its rich aromas wafting around me.

I have missed this for the forty-plus years I have lived in New York City.

There was a time in my earlier life that I would travel to the suburban Philadelphia home of my college buddy JD and help him plant his garden each spring. We would spend the weekends together and honestly have a grand time planting, reminiscing, and laughing, followed by a great meal prepared on his grill. This was always accompanied by a bottle of Brolio wine from the Castello di Brolio vineyard and winery we visited in Italy, and were lucky enough to find in his local wine store. Teri and Kerry, who traveled to Italy with us, were always present for these meals enjoyed outdoors on JD's deck. I always packed an old pair of jeans, as I knew the knees of these jeans would be caked with dirt from being on my hands and knees in his garden. I would return several times during the summer to either watch the progress, or be there to celebrate the first ripe tomatoes, which were later, always the featured center of our dinners.

My mom and dad were avid gardeners. For that matter, so was everyone in my childhood neighborhood, as well as all of my uncles and aunts. There was usually a competition as to who would have the first ripe tomato each year. One year, my dad was determined to win, so he planted his tomatoes in March. It was still the end of winter, and frost was almost guaranteed if there wasn't snow. I was given the assignment of covering the tomato plants each night, so the cold would not damage them, and uncovering them before school each morning. This was hardly a chore for me. I, too, was actively a part of the competition.

I learned gentleness in gardening from my mother, who would tend her gardens each day. I can still hear her words, "Watch you don't break the stems or step on the plants," as she taught a young me her gardening skills. Her annual petunias or portulacas, planted in the raised garden bed between our back porch and the sidewalk that paralleled it, were legendary. They often grew and flowered over the sidewalk and forced guests to walk on the adjacent grass rather than use the sidewalk. My cousins still talk about them.

Mom and Dad's generation grew up during a time of required Victory Gardens during World War II and gardens providing the food for almost all of their families' meals during the Great Depression. Dad often told me stories about him and his younger sister Ruth tending their family gardens each morning before going to school and each night before starting their homework by the light of an oil lamp.

There are many, many family stories centered on my grandpap Bernini's garden; many of them are still vivid, generations later, among us cousins. Grandma Bernini had a peony bush that she cherished. Grandpap Bernini would joke that "you can't eat it, so what good is it?" I believe Mom took that peony bush with her when she and Dad sold my grandparents' home after the passing of my grandparents. I say that because there was a beautiful peony bush in the backyard of our two-story home on Walnut Street in Black Lick when I was a kid. Mom tended to it lovingly. I often wonder why she did not take it when my parents sold that house and moved to their 1960s ranch-style home. Unfortunately, I never thought to ask Mom while she was still with us in this life.

***

The sunflowers of my morning walks continued to grow. I watched them bud then burst into their beautiful blooms. Sunflowers are very happy flowers. They will make you smile, no matter your mood. Perhaps this is one of their purposes in life. I was delighted for these sunflowers, surviving and thriving as they did in an urn on First Avenue in Manhattan, and not far from my home. I assume that life in an urn on First Avenue is not an easy life, so I gave these sunflowers a lot of credit for their survival.

And I would stop each morning and talk to them, often praising them for their beauty. Yes, I do this with plants. They are made up of cells, just as we are. And I believe they have emotions, just as we do, but a "plant form" of emotions. I've read many times that talking to plants can enhance their well-being. Often, as I was a block or two away and they came into sight, I would be eager to arrive at their urn to see their progress. The sunflowers and I formed a relationship. Perhaps they felt me approaching.

But—yes, there is a but in this story—one morning I arrived to find one of the flowers missing. It had been severed from its stem. I assumed someone then had it in a vase in their apartment. I was annoyed, but I wasn't surprised. I knew not everyone shared the same type of enthusiasm for these beautiful survivors that I did. And then, on another day, another of the sunflowers had its stem broken, and the flower had drooped to the side of its stem. Horrors. Clearly someone tried to remove the sunflower from its stem, but thought they could do it by twisting the stem off. They naturally failed, as sunflowers have extraordinarily strong stems. But worst, they just left it there, hanging.

I did try to console it with comforting words.

Think I am a little looney? Well, that sunflower with the broken stem started to right itself over the next weeks. Yes, it eventually was back to its full length, stretching itself toward the sun, as sunflowers do. Its stem had been damaged and was now scarred, but, like humans, its cells worked to repair itself. I was very happy for it. I encouraged and congratulated it. Another story of survival in the Big Apple.

The spring in my steps resumed as I approached the urn of sunflowers each morning. It remained for a few weeks.

One day, as I approached the urn, I saw from a distance that the sunflowers were all gone. Only severed stems remained. Unbelievable. Someone stole all the sunflowers. I say stole because that is how I felt.

I was heartsick.

They were a thing of beauty amid a vast stretch of concrete abutting three blocks of vacant lots. For me, this beautiful urn of sunflowers gave me the sense of working the soil again. They brought me back to my Western Pennsylvania farm-country roots of gardening. Although I never touched the soil or the sunflowers, as someone else had planted them, they filled, in their own way, a void I had in my life for working the soil.

A few weeks later, the urn was filled with plastic bottles and candy wrappers, all sitting around the stems of the sunflowers, which by now, were dying. As I gently touched their dying stems, I thanked them for what they meant to me and wished them well.

Steam Pipes and Peter Pan

Many know that I try to take a two-mile walk each morning before starting work when I am working from home. This is my time to relax into the day, think about what I need to accomplish for work, compose email responses in my mind, and so on. It is also a time to relax my mind as I take in the morning, rain or shine.

Yesterday as I was walking up Second Avenue, I was stopped at Fifty-First Street. Fire trucks, firemen, police cars, and officers were everywhere. Second Avenue was cordoned off for several blocks. I was diverted to First Avenue to continue my walk to the Italian Market I now frequent since the one in my neighborhood closed after one hundred-plus years of operation. I stopped to ask a construction worker what happened. A steam pipe exploded under Fifty-Second Street the previous night. No one was hurt, but the damage was extensive. The remnants of the foam firefighters use to extinguish fires was everywhere.

I heard on the local news last night that the residents in the area were advised to keep their windows closed due to the possibility of the air being contaminated with asbestos.

When I arrived home after yesterday's walk, I found a woman dressed as a princess in the lobby of our building.

She was highly decked out as royalty from a fairy tale. She was talking to David, one of the doormen. She had a look of distress on her face. Princesses are not to have looks of distress. I was intrigued. I nodded to David and the princess. I walked on toward the elevator, quickly ending eye contact, as most New Yorkers do, and of course avoiding engagement that may lead to conversation, as most New Yorkers do.

Today on my two-mile walk, I was again diverted at Fifty-First Street. The fire trucks, firemen, police cars, and officers were still there. Cleanup had begun. There were also a lot of repairs beginning.

When I returned to the lobby of my building after my walk, I asked David about the princess with whom he was talking the previous day. She was an actor, employed to play ALL the characters from the movie *Frozen* for a children's party in the community room on the fourth floor of my building. At that point, she was dressed as a princess. But she was turned away at the door of the party. Apparently some parents objected to a woman playing the part of the prince in *Frozen*. David told me that the parents didn't want their young boys to see a woman playing the part of a man. David shrugged his shoulders. Her contract was cancelled at that moment. She never got inside of the community room, even as a woman dressed as a princess.

I live in New York City. I've seen a lot. I have come to accept a lot and ignore a lot. My dad once called me years ago when the local news back in Western Pennsylvania had a segment on a very large man dressed in drag who was a noted bouncer at a noted nightclub. Dad wanted to know if I lived anywhere near the nightclub. I didn't. He seemed to be concerned that I didn't find this alarming. By then, I had been in New York for fifteen years or so. No, not alarming. Steam pipe explosions and asbestos are alarming. I wasn't judging my dad's concern.

David and I discussed why a woman playing a prince mattered. We were both bewildered. Let's see...Shakespeare had men playing the parts of women. Would little boys really experience gender confusion from a young woman playing a prince at a party?

I leave you with one thought—who really was Peter Pan?

Quiet

I am back with my client in Mexico City. It is Saturday morning. I am spending two consecutive weeks here during this engagement. Prior to the global pandemic, I always spent two consecutive weeks with my client in Mexico City. Since the pandemic, I alternate weeks. Between the airfare and the weekend hotel rates, the cost is about the same as when I stayed two consecutive weeks. Plus, it gives me more flexibility for scheduling my other clients.

I had a very busy week last week at work. Don't let anyone tell you anything different; business travel is about long hours and little leisure time. If you are fortunate, there is a good restaurant in the hotel for a relaxing meal and a glass of wine at the end of most days. I tend to return to my rooms at night with enough time to prepare for bed. Given this, I don't mind the long hours and the travel; I am fortunate to love my work.

This morning, I woke later after a great night of consecutive hours of sleep. At the Intercontinental here in Mexico City, I learned early on to request a room facing the city, not Chapultepec Park, Mexico City's equivalent of New York City's Central Park. Chapultepec Park is the largest and oldest park in Latin America, a verdant forest of paths and lakes and beautiful flowers and sculptures, artfully and architecturally designed for leisure. Between the hotel, though, and the park is the Auditorio Nacional, where many international stars and music groups perform. The Dave Matthews Band was recently here, as was Il Volo from Italy; Diana Krall will soon perform there. After the performances, late at night the noise of the audiences leaving this venue can sound like midnight in Times Square on New Year's Eve. The city side of the hotel is virtually quiet. And dark.

I remained in bed for a long time this morning. I allowed the silence and the darkness to envelop me. It was intentional. I kept my mind from wandering into those places that consume my days. I love early mornings like this and looked forward to them while spending weekends at the Intercontinental when I was working here prior to the pandemic. Trust me, not every Saturday morning is like this. I often do awake with a million things on my mind, leftovers from the day before or something that surfaced while I was sleeping. I do cherish the silence, however. And the darkness. While choosing to be a resident of New York City, these are not among the benefits of living there.

There is certainly something calming about starting a day with silence and early morning darkness. I find I tend to move slower. My thoughts are more contemplative. My movements are more deliberate. I don't suddenly find myself dressed and on my way to work, wondering if I turned off the lights.

I am often envious when I hear from my friend Rita as she is texting or calling me while having coffee on her front porch back in Western Pennsylvania. Rita says she is "having coffee on my porch," not that she is "going to have coffee on my porch." The phrase "going to have coffee on my porch" sounds more directional, more intentional than the ease of just "having coffee on my porch." And knowing Rita, I know she is there, moving slower, more deliberately, and more contemplatively.

She has shared photos of her yard during those calm morning-coffee moments. Once, she sent a photo of an incredibly intricate and beautiful spiderweb, the creation of a little spider who was busy the entire prior night, weaving this piece of nature's wonderment. But Rita's text that morning wasn't about an alarming moment of an unexpected spider and its web on her porch; it was of a moment of contemplating nature's beauty while sipping coffee during the silence of the early morning hours of crisp country air and a rising sun.

And I am reminded often of my neighbors Edith and Joe when I was growing up in Edgemont. Mom often sat my baby brother in his high chair facing the dining room window so Bob could watch the activities in the nearby yards as she busied herself with work around our home. Joe was often working in his yard during these times; "Joe" became my brother's first word. Bob had trouble pronouncing "Edith" when he was learning to talk; her name came out as "Elee." We have called her Elee since.

In the summer, when Dad fired up our outdoor grill, Elee and Joe often joined us for impromptu dinners on our patio. At that time, this wasn't known as "dining alfresco." Elee and Joe were always invited without deliberate invitation. Joe, being a butcher, often contributed incredible cuts of meat or chicken from the local market he owned with Elee's brother, Ed. We'd sit outdoors, relaxed and enjoying the main course together with the side dishes Mom and Elee prepared; too soon another outdoor shared dinner was over.

Elee was like a second mother to my brother and me, and we often enjoyed her Italian cooking and pastries. During summers, Elee had a dedicated evening routine. After dinner each evening, she sat quietly on her back porch, which faced ours, and either read, crocheted, or knitted, completely absorbed. Her favorite books were about La Cosa Nostra. She once knitted a beautiful sculpted ivory-wool throw for me as a Christmas gift. I still have it. It must weigh ten pounds. When I use it, I am reminded of Elee's quiet time on her back porch. Her moment to herself of chosen silence, complete relaxation, and total contemplation of her own thoughts.

As I grow older, I find the silence to be something I look forward to experiencing when I can do so. Those calm early mornings in bed before the world around me starts to move were first relished by me when I was in college. With my roommate still asleep in his bed, I absorbed the silence. The nonstop need to study, to listen intently in classes while taking notes at the speed of light, to overachieve in my grades, to attend a party believing it was a way to relax while music blared around me as I participated in mindless conversation three decibels above my normal voice level—this all contributed to my first appreciation of the silence of early morning hours. It also made me appreciate how my mind during those moments could relax itself into a pleasant blank space of no thoughts, no worries, no cares.

Life for me sped up after college. Grad school, work, career, bills, life and trying to take it all in and keep up took control of me, as it did for many of us. Those early morning hours faded into a distant memory for me for many, many years. During that time, though, like my mother, I found that pausing to read before going to bed was a way to shut out the day that was just behind me and take my mind off the day that was just in front of me.

I enjoy reading about history and the biographies of notable people. Mom enjoyed biographies of celebrities and the First Ladies of the United States. Sometimes as Mom was reading on the love seat in our living room, she would put the book down and just stare into space. I never thought about this action of hers until I found myself doing the same one night years ago as I was reading. I was thinking about what I had just read. Perhaps Mom was doing the same. My eyes were no longer looking at a page of words in a book; my mind had taken over and was exploring those sequences of phrases recorded by the author of a time, a place, a person in whom I had an interest. Eventually, I closed the book and just began allowing my mind to slow down for the night.

I still read before bed. The room must be dim, and I try to achieve silence as best I can while living in New York City. Some nights I read many pages or even a chapter; other nights it is only a few paragraphs. Like Pavlov's dogs, it triggers my mind that the day is soon to be over. Before falling asleep, I stop to enjoy the silence, the quiet of the moment. This is my treat.

I believe silence is a gift we have been given, one which we may not fully appreciate. The quiet of a moment or of an hour or two is restorative, not only to our bodies, but more importantly to our minds. My dad often told me that it is easy to rest your body, but it is difficult to rest your mind. The conscious act of remaining quiet and listening to the silence, perhaps, is what he did so many evenings while sitting in his easy chair before going to bed. It is what I do now.

Pearl Harbor

I always wonder where my mom and dad were and what they were doing on this day, December 7, 1941, the day the United States was attacked at Pearl Harbor. The time there was 7:55 a.m.; the time on the East Coast where Mom and Dad were was 12:55 p.m. It was a Sunday. They were probably arriving home from Saint Bonaventure Church and the Methodist church, their respective churches, in our then-bustling little hometown of Black Lick. Or perhaps having their large midday Sunday family dinners.

Mom was fourteen years old, a freshman in high school. Dad was three days away from turning nineteen years old. He had graduated from Blairsville High the previous year and was working. There wasn't twenty-four-seven news back then. The news came over radios in their living rooms. Although Dad's sister Ruth and Mom's sister Della were friends, Mom and Dad had not yet met.

I often wonder what their reactions were when they heard the news. Dad was of conscription age for the army. Mom had four older brothers, all who could be eligible for service. Two grandmas and two grandpaps had to be hand-wringing, worried when the United States declared war on Japan, and then on December 11 declared war on Germany. Two battle fronts.

By then, the US had its share of Hitler Youth camps spread around the country, where indoctrinations were taking place among some of our youth. Too, our Congress had its share of Nazi sympathizers who were touting Nazism and isolationism to keep the US out of the war in Europe. Later, it was discovered that many of these initiatives in our country were being secretly funded by monies from Hitler in his well-planned strategy to cause discord and disunity in our country and to raise sympathy for his cause. By 1941, Poland, France, and the Benelux countries had fallen to Hitler. People who were considered inferior were being sent to "camps." German subs were patrolling the East Coast of the US. Yes, read your history.

So, my parents…what were you thinking on December 7, 1941, when the news about Pearl Harbor came across the radios in your parents' living rooms? What were your reactions? What were you doing? The sense of ease from your church services may have been overwhelmed by these events.

Did you even think another world war would emerge from this Sunday just a few weeks away from your Christmas celebrations?

I wish I had known to ask.

Mrs. Byron

I received a text, from my friend Nancy, informing me that Mrs. Byron passed away. She was ninety-nine years old. She was also our grade school music teacher. She is not to be confused with our grade school band teacher, Mr. Mruk.

I read Mrs. Byron's obituary. It stated that:

> She taught in the Blairsville and State College Area School Districts, retiring in 1984 after a career as an elementary general music teacher.

Nancy and I agreed she was much more.

My recollections of Mrs. Byron begin in third grade. She may have taught my classes in first and second grades, but those memories, if they exist, are buried deep in my subconscious now.

Music was around our home long before I started going to school, though. As many moms of that era, my mom often sang to me. I remember her teaching me the song "Mairzy Doats (and Dozy Doats)" and "A Bushel and a Peck." And Mom and Dad had a blond-wood 1960s mid-century modern hi-fi on which Dad often played their favorite record albums.

I had a record too at that time. It was a narrative of *The Little Engine that Could.*

When kindergarten came around, and I finally stopped crying and let go of my mom on that first day, music suddenly became a sing-along event for me. Our teacher, Mrs. George, would play songs on her seafoam-green upright piano as we all sat around her on the floor and performed "Old MacDonald Had a Farm," "Frère Jacques," or sequentially sang "Row, Row, Row Your Boat" as only a roomful of five-year-olds could do. Once, we had to choose a circus animal to imitate; then Mrs. George played circus music while we paraded around the room, imitating our chosen animal. But I digressed...

Third grade opened a new world for me. Nancy, whom I've known since kindergarten, and I started writing poetry together—yes, third-grade poets. We were suddenly no longer learning to write cursive while staying inside the lines of the paper, but learning geography and history and math in a much different way. That year, too, we studied the metric system in anticipation of the United States converting over, but as we now know, this never happened. And it is then that my recollections of Mrs. Byron become vivid.

Our young minds didn't realize at the time the efforts she took to coordinate our music lessons with our studies. When first learning about the Revolutionary War, Mrs. Byron taught us the song "Yankee Doodle." When first studying the Civil War, we sang "When Johnny Comes Marching Home."

In fourth grade, for Veteran's Day, Mrs. Byron had us sing the anthems of all the branches of the military. And, that year, when studying European countries in geography, we sang "*Santa Lucia*" among other country-centric songs.

Mrs. Byron must have had a blast while listening to all our young voices, and probably hoping most of us could stay on key. During holidays, she had us sing the usual songs, one of which still resonates with me—"Over the River and Through the Woods," which we sang at Thanksgiving. I recently read this was written as a poem by Lydia Maria Child in 1844 and published in her book of children's poetry, *Flowers for Children*. I remember trudging home from grade school on the Wednesdays before Thanksgiving, snow on the ground, this song rolling around in my head as I anticipated the next day's feast. We had snow on the ground at Thanksgiving then in Western Pennsylvania. Simpler times.

As I've listened to children's choirs in church, their collective voices have an angelic quality about them. I wonder if Mrs. Byron felt this as she moved from room to room in Burrell Elementary School, teaching her music lessons and having her pupils' voices wash over her. Children's voices are magical, and this had to have been one of the many rewards of her teaching career.

Mrs. Byron was a gentlewoman of joy. She always had a smile on her face, a pitch pipe in hand, and folders filled with sheets of music as she entered our classroom. She would put the folders down on our homeroom-teacher's desk and begin her lesson with us, still smiling. Every day was a new adventure in song with her.

My third-grade teacher, Mrs. Pitzerell, was in her twenties. She had platinum-blonde hair, dressed very 1960s mod, and was very pretty, but not as pretty as my mom. Mrs. Bruggemann, my fourth-grade teacher who was also in her twenties, was a Bobbie Jo to Mrs. Pitzerell's Billie Jo. Another natural beauty but dressed more conservatively. Both always had smiles on their faces, too. Both got an hour break from us when Mrs. Byron entered our classrooms. Mrs. Byron had to have spent time working with both of them on their lesson plans to coordinate music with our studies.

While Mrs. Pitzerell and Mrs. Bruggemann were teaching us reading comprehension and how to read without moving our lips, Mrs. Byron had the daunting task of teaching us to add another dimension to our reading—musical notes. She taught our young minds to understand the meaning and use of whole notes and half notes, how to watch her for signals to sing softly or sing loudly, and when to stop singing when she gave the direction with her hands.

But there was also a more abstract lesson for our young minds within her lessons. She was teaching us to engage our minds on multiple levels simultaneously: we had to read a word on a page, attach it to a note that signaled both how the word should sound and how long to "hold" it, and we had to watch her hand motions for signals, all at the same time. Four full dimensions…

Four full dimensions times thirty students times three third- and fourth-grade homerooms and two fifth-grade homerooms in my elementary school times a lifetime of teaching, all while keeping her students' voices on key.

Eventually, Nancy's family moved to State College. Mrs. Byron had moved there earlier. Nancy kept in touch with Mrs. Byron over the years. I was excited to receive a video from Nancy of one of her visits with Mrs. Byron several years ago. It opened a window in my mind that had been closed for years—actually, I had forgotten that what was on the other side of that window even existed. Suddenly it was the day before Thanksgiving, and I was walking home from grade school in the snow, humming "Over the River..."

Mrs. Byron was foundational to hundreds, if not thousands, of her students' education in music, helping some of us eventually to stay on key as we sang to the radios in our cars, allowing many of us to join church choirs and many to still remember the lyrics of the military anthems we once sang in unison. And for some, she germinated a seed that would lead to PhD degrees and careers in music. But to all of us, she was a wonderful teacher who helped us learn to engage our young minds simultaneously on multiple levels while teaching us music.

I like to think that perhaps Mrs. Byron is now in heaven with a choir of angel children in front of her, pitch pipe in hand, ready to give the downbeat to the song "Santa Lucia," eager once again to hear angelic voices lifted in unison as she did so many times for so many years as our beloved grade school music teacher.

Yes, perhaps.

Questions Not Asked

Nineteen fifty-one (1951)was a big year for weddings for Mom and Dad's circle of friends and family, with cousin Betty Lou and Ray's wedding in May and the wedding of Mom and Dad's close friends Irene and Punchy later in August. But for Mom and Dad, the event of the year was their own marriage on February 3.

Mom and Dad were married in Saint Bonaventure Church, the Roman Catholic church of my mom's family, located in my childhood hometown of Black Lick, Pennsylvania. I have lots of photos of Mom and Dad's wedding, both formal and candid. Mom and Dad were smiling in all of them, most notably with their eyes. There is a wonderful photo of them exiting the church and walking down the long flight of steps in front of Saint Bonaventure to the car waiting to whisk the newlyweds off to their reception. It is a favorite photo of mine. There was a major snowstorm that day, and Mom often commented that if you look closely at that photo, the tips of the calla lilies she carried are brown from the frigid cold.

I wonder what Dad was thinking as his best man, my uncle Mario, and he walked down the aisle to the altar of Saint Bonaventure to await Mom's arrival. I wonder what exchange they may have had. It probably wasn't a lot of conversation, as in those days you didn't talk in church. But there had to be eye exchanges and some side whispers. I wonder what Dad thought as he exchanged glances with his mother who was in a front pew. And I suspect Uncle Mario, the tease that he was, poked my dad once or twice in the ribs to elicit a smile from the nervous groom as they stood there. Uncle Mario was married to Mom's older sister Della. He and Aunt Della had a three-year-old cutie of a daughter named Nancy Lee, who preceded Mom down the aisle as her flower girl.

Mom chose to have a formal wedding, so she was dressed in a full-length gown. Once, when my brother and I were young, she pulled her wedding gown, veil, and train out of the cedar chest, which was once her hope chest given to her by her brother Charles, my uncle Keck. Mom put it on. The train was easily twelve feet in length or longer, and when laid out from her dress, it extended almost the entire length of the hallway of the bedroom area of the home in which we were then living. I remember my mom looking beautiful that day.

Climbing that long flight of steps on a snowy day in full wedding dress and train must have been a challenge, but I know she was assisted by her matron of honor—Mom's oldest sister, Inez, whom everyone called Giggi. And on the other side of her was her brother Reno, who gave Mom away. Aunt Giggi was dressed in a lavender gown and headpiece. Lavender was the favorite color of my mom's mother, my grandma Bernini. Grandma Bernini, whom the family called Mama, passed suddenly two years prior, and Mom and Dad had postponed their marriage to observe a respectful period of mourning. My granddad Pap was, as was the entire family, greatly shaken by Grandma's sudden and unexpected passing in her sleep. Pap, as I have been told, never recovered from losing "my Maria."

I wonder what Mom was thinking as she climbed those steps to the front door of Saint Bonaventure. I wonder what she felt as she entered the church filled with family and friends and saw Dad standing there in front of the altar decorated in white roses, waiting for her to be escorted down the aisle. I am sure it was a moment of overload of sights and emotions as she took it all in. I wonder if she had butterflies as she watched the roll of white fabric on which she would walk to the altar being slowly unfurled down the aisle. I wonder, too, what she felt when she took Uncle Reno's arm as the organ music commenced, and as Aunt Giggi started down the aisle in lockstep, then Nancy Lee, and now Mom with her dear brother Reno. I am sure she looked up at Uncle Reno along the way, Uncle Reno who bought Mom her high school ring and whose shoes Mom polished as a young girl before his dates with his future wife, my aunt Marian. I am sure Mom nodded in a teary smile to Pap who was in the front pew. I am sure she nodded and smiled at Grandma Olson seated across from Pap.

I wish I would have known to ask questions when Mom and Dad were still with us, but I believe it takes age and wisdom to realize what you don't know…and what you realize you want to know.

Dad converted to Catholicism from his Methodist religion, which resulted in a bit of a stir back in that time. His seven sisters bought him the suit for his wedding.

Mom had planned for him to wear a tuxedo, but the heartfelt gift of Dad's seven sisters was respected. Mom's childhood home sat next to the home of the Colesar family. Mrs. Colesar was one of Grandma Bernini's best friends, and stories abound as to how they would sit together on their back porches during summer evenings, talking while crocheting and embroidering or snapping beans and peas from their gardens. Mrs. Colesar's youngest daughter, nick-named Tootie (everyone seemed to have nicknames back then), was Mom's best friend when she was growing up. I have a very sweet picture of Mom and Tootie, each about seven years old, sitting together in their white dresses and veiled crowns on the day of their First Holy Communion at Saint Bonaventure Church.

Mrs. Colesar was a seamstress; she made Mom's wed-ding gown, veil, headpiece, and train. It included intricate beaded embellishments. As stated in Mom and Dad's wedding announcement in the local newspaper:

> *The bride...was beautiful in a gown of white*
> *slipper satin fashioned with a round neckline*
> *and yoke of chiffon, long pointed sleeves and a*
> *long full skirt ending in a train. Her veil fell*
> *from a crown of beaded sapphires.*

Mrs. Colesar made it all.

That morning, I wonder what Mom was thinking as her sisters Giggi, Nellie, and Della assisted their younger sister, the last of the family to marry. Was she excited? Was she nervous? What did she have for breakfast? Did she sleep the night before? I am sure the sisters stopped in a moment of silent prayer to remember their mama. When Mom departed her childhood home for the last time as a single woman, what did she say to her father, our pap? Did he ride with her in the car to the church?

And all the same questions come to mind as I think of my dad. What did his sisters say as he debuted his wedding suit, the one that they lovingly pooled their money together to buy for him? No doubt my dear grandma Olson shed a few tears as she hugged her firstborn child, the son who, as the eldest and together with his sister Ruth, diligently rode the waves of the Great Depression with her to support their eight younger siblings.

Mom and Dad's reception was celebrated in the main event hall of the Central Hotel, which was owned by Aunt Della and Uncle Mario. There is a wonderful photo that includes my aunt Marian, Uncle Reno's wife, carrying my mom's bouquet of calla lilies.

No doubt an Italian dinner was served that day. I have a photo of my dad's family all sitting together during dinner, his two brothers and seven sisters, and Grandma. His oldest sister, Ruth, his soulmate in their younger lives, and her husband, John, had a prominent place at the table. And I have in my parents' photo albums a touching photo of Mom hugging Pap. Their cheeks are touching as they are smiling and looking a bit teary. The photo is iconic of a father and his youngest daughter on the day of her wedding. Both, no doubt, were simultaneously holding a very dear memory of their wife and mother at that moment. I believe Mama was there, though, looking down on them and smiling a teary smile of her own.

And surrounding Pap and Mom in that photo were some of my female cousins, just young kids at the time and looking cute as buttons: Diana, Donna Jean, and, of course, Nancy Lee. My cousin Phyllis was there, too. She was eleven at the time and once shared with me how beautiful my mom was as she was escorted down the aisle earlier in the day by Uncle Reno.

The last photo that I have of Mom and Dad's wedding day was taken before leaving on their honeymoon. Mom was wearing her new "going away" suit with matching hat and gloves; Dad still looked spiffy in his suit from the wedding. Both are smiling in one of those "Kodak moment" photos.

What were they thinking as that photo was taken, departing their families now as a couple, leaving behind the freedom of singledom, knowing that the life ahead of them, an unknown life, would unfold among the familiar and unfamiliar?

Were my brother and I yet a twinkle in their eyes?

All questions never asked, the answers to which are now staring at me, but tightly locked within fading black-and-white photographs.

Separated at Ten

My fifth-grade teacher, Mr. Coup, rearranged the desks in our classroom so that the entire class was sitting two by two. Mr. Coup paired my cousin Chuck with me, explaining that we were cousins and, as such, should sit together. We were smack in the middle of the room, the third set of desks back from the front of the classroom, in the middle row. It was an excellent location.

Chuck was whip-smart. I remember him arriving one morning to tell me he didn't study for the test that day. My eyes had to have shown alarm. I am sure he aced the test. I once asked him how he was always the first to finish tests AND get As on them. He just looked at me and smiled. As cousins, we were competitive with each other, but we had mutual respect for our accomplishments, as we both worked hard to achieve our grades together.

One morning, Mr. Coup grabbed a twelve-inch wooden ruler from his desk, barreled down the aisle, lifted Chuck's left hand, and started smacking it with the ruler. I have no recollection as to why this happened. Chuck held back his tears, but his face was red with emotional and physical pain. The class was stunned. I was angry. I wanted to grab that ruler from Mr. Coup and break it in half. He was hitting my cousin!

I am sure Mr. Coup had no idea he was actually striking out at not one, but two boys of strong Italian heritage—two cousins at the same time—by hitting just one of them. Two young Italian boys who had not fully gained control of their Italian anger. Two young Italian boys who had learned early that "family is family," and "you don't mess with family."

Chuck and I remained silent, however, as our young blood pressures rose off the charts. I wish I could say it was a lesson about something Chuck had done, but it wasn't. For me, it was a lesson of how much I loved my cousin, and as an extension of him, how the bonds of family were rooting themselves in my young mind.

Better sense took me over, however, before I reacted against Mr. Coup, as my dad's oft-repeated phrase reminded me that if I got into trouble at school, expect the punishment to continue at home. I suspect Chuck had heard the same thing from Uncle Keck.

Still, my cousin hurt. And so did I...for him.

***

Chuck lived one block from me when my family still lived in the two-story, yellow-clapboard house on Walnut Street in Black Lick. Chuckie's family home was on Main Street. It was another large home built during another era when

Black Lick was a booming industrial and coal-mining town supporting the steel mills of Pittsburgh. His home had a finished attic where his oldest sister, Marlene, could roller-skate.

Mom would watch me as I walked to Chuckie's home to play with him. We moved out of the two-story, yellow-clapboard house when I had just turned six, so there was a reason for Mom to watch me as I walked to Chuckie's house. To get there, I traveled across the backyard of our neighbors, the Gearys; through the backyard of the Presbyterian Church; past Mr. and Mrs. George's glazed cinder-block garage; past the back of the Sugar Bowl, the local confectionary; and on to Chuckie's backyard. I suspect Chuckie's mother, my aunt Helen, was watching for me, too, as I made those walks. It was a more genteel time in life back then. In total, Chuckie's home was only about three blocks away from ours, but I am not sure parents would even consider a five-year-old walking three blocks alone any longer.

Chuckie's family lived in a house we could explore. It was large. His three older sisters were never home, and his mother was always busy, so we would wander around the house, checking the second-floor rooms just to see how they looked, but perhaps, too, just checking to see if we could find something that would interest two five-year-old boys. Their home had a small backyard where his Dad, my uncle Keck, had erected a swing set. As kids, we all knew swing sets were good for only a period of time, but then, after much swinging and sliding, it was time to move on to something else to do in the yard or elsewhere.

Unfortunately, his yard was too small to even bat a ball around.

On the far end of their dining room was a set of French doors that opened to Uncle Keck's office. I remember that his desk was always piled high with papers. The office had a window that looked out to their backyard, where Chuckie and I played.

Before Mom was married, she was the business manager for Uncle Keck's mining and foundry businesses. Mom always had stories about managing Uncle Keck's businesses, some of which I may write about someday. The work brought them closer as brother and sister, but then, my mom was the youngest of eight siblings. She was the "baby" and the darling of all her siblings throughout her life.

I am fortunate to have two Aunt Helens—one on Mom's side, one on Dad's side; both are great cooks. I heard from my cousins that Chuckie's mother learned all her cooking skills from Grandma Bernini. Similar to our home at that time, Chuckie's home had a very large kitchen with a breakfast nook. Aunt Helen's kitchen cabinets were made of wood and painted a shade of green reminiscent of the 1940s. The cabinets had decals on them. I don't remember the details of the decals, but I do remember Aunt Helen's cooking.

Aunt Helen sometimes permitted Chuckie to come up to my yard to play on my swing set and in my sandbox. I have several noteworthy photos of Chuckie, our cousin Marla, and me on that swing set. Of the three of us, I was the smallest. Mom always had a hat on my head to cover my ears since I had a lot of earaches as a kid. In the photos, it is summer, and I am wearing earmuffs.

***

When we moved to our new ranch-style home in Edgemont, Chuckie and I were no longer in walking distance of each other. We were now in biking distance of each other. Due to the distance, we spent less time together. Plus, Uncle Keck started taking my young cousin Chuckie on his rounds to inspect his businesses during the summers. Clearly, this was to introduce his only son to managing the coal-mining and foundry businesses someday.

Chuck was fascinated with his dad's coal mines and the coal-mining process. Once, when I rode my bike to his home, he asked me if I wanted to see "his" coal mine. I was game. We went to a vacant lot nearby, in the middle of which lay a large piece of plywood. Chuck pulled the plywood back, and there was a hole in the ground. Not just a "hole," but a huge, dark, foreboding hole that led into a huge, dark, foreboding tunnel. The hole was easily eight feet deep or more. I could peer into the tunnel from the hole. The tunnel was long and dark. Nowhere to be found was the excavated dirt, however, from the digging Chuck and another friend had spent weeks doing.

Yes, my cousin Chuck had dug a "coal mine." Chuck asked me if I wanted to go inside to see it. I was quick to decline. I can still see the moment I turned down his belowground adventure. He looked puzzled. I guess I would have too, had I dug a "coal mine." But descending into that hole did not hold any interest for me, neither did whatever may be living in it.

Later, I heard Uncle Keck learned of Chuckie's coal mine and had some of the miners from his company fill in the tunnel and hole. I can only guess what may have happened the night Uncle Keck learned of that "coal mine."

***

While living in our new house, there was a knock at our back door one evening, and in walked Chuckie. Mom wasn't home at the time. Chuckie sat down in my usual seat at the far end of our kitchen table and folded his hands on his lap. His face was a sea of distress; his body, tense. Something had happened to him, and our home was the closest relative's "safe house." I don't fully remember the incident that precipitated this moment. That is Chuck's story to tell. But there he sat, anguished, his shoulders heaving with each breath. Dad worked to comfort him and understand the nature of what just happened.

I had come into the kitchen as soon as I heard my cousin Chuck's voice and had sat down at the other end of the table. I immediately felt his distress in my own being. I remember my eight- or nine-year-old heart ached for my cousin. Ached as his may have ached at that moment. It was all the raw emotion of youth, emotion that had not yet been tempered by years of experience, years of learning how to manage aches of the heart. Something happened to my cousin, and I was feeling it with him.

I was too young to understand at the time that I was feeling the deep-rooted bonds of family, that bridge of DNA and culture and history and unquestioning love that exists among family members. But, too, this moment took the bond one step deeper, in that Chuck and I were the same age, contemporaries and friends, all sitting on top of our foundational DNA and culture and history. To this day, I still see that moment, I still feel that moment, and I still hold Chuck in my heart as that moment unveiled itself in front of me. It was the beginning of understanding that family is family. Family is family. Period.

***

Living in Edgemont, after we moved from our two-story, yellow-clapboard home, I was closer in proximity to my cousin Marla. I know we were in the same playpen together when we were young. Her mother and my mom were the two youngest siblings in their family; they had a special bond that continued throughout their lives. As sisters, they shared all things girls share when they are young; this continued throughout their lives. So it was natural that Marla and I would grow close as the years progressed.

Marla's home was at the base of a great hill in Edgemont. The land on the hill was once owned by the Campbell Farm in Grafton and was planted with field corn each year by the Campbells. After the harvesting season was finished and the great snowfalls of Western Pennsylvania began, the hill was Marla's and my go-to hill for sled riding. Bundled beyond the ability to easily walk or move our arms, we would drag our sleds almost to the top of the hill, and whether sitting on our sleds or lying on them, we always had a thrilling ride, stopping just short of Blaire Road, which was at the base of the hill.

So, one snowy, wintry day, Marla and I took my red sled to the top of the hill. I lay down on it, and Marla lay on top of me, and off we went, picking up the desired speed we loved. My steering, however, wasn't so great that day, and as we approached the bottom of the hill, we were headed straight into the back of Marla's red-brick house... We crashed straight into a basement window. Fortunately, the metal frame of the window stopped my sled. Unfortunately, Aunt Della heard the impact and the cracking of glass and came running out of her house to see what happened. I had to go home that day and take my sled with me. Marla's riding for the day was over too.

Marla and I spent a lot of time together as kids. When younger and playing indoors during inclement-weather days, I was always told that I was going to be the "father" when Marla wanted to play house. Being the father meant pushing the baby buggy, with her Chatty Cathy doll in it, as we "went for a walk" or "went shopping" or whatever came into the mind of a young girl. My job was to push and wait, sometimes take Chatty out of the buggy, sometimes just watch her. I didn't mind. Marla was my cousin, and we were playing.

The way Chatty spoke didn't hold much interest for me. I suspected it was a recorder of some sort. But there was the episode of Marla's new doll that Santa brought her, a doll whose hair, if you pushed a button on her stomach, grew. When visiting soon after Christmas, Marla was eager to take me to her bedroom to show me her new doll. As I watched her demonstrate the hair growth and retraction, I suggested we take the doll apart to see how it worked. So Marla trustingly let me disassemble the new doll that Santa brought her. It is needless to write about the outcome. I could not put the doll back together again, Marla was more than upset, Aunt Della and Uncle Mario were more than upset, and Mom and Dad were furious. They took me home.

I don't remember what happened next, but I do remember that I had to empty my piggy bank to pay for the doll. Mom and Dad took me to a local toy store and told me I had to buy a new doll for Marla, one that was exactly like the hair-growing doll I disassembled. As I started to get out of the car, Mom and Dad explained they were not going into the store with me. I was on my own to buy the doll. This was my punishment.

So there I was, in the doll aisle of the toy store, picking out the doll and carrying it to the checkout counter, then emptying my pockets of small bills and loose change. I was worried my friends—well, anyone really—would see me buying a doll. It is another scene in life that I cannot forget. I never took another doll apart. Ever.

I was at home in Marla's house, and Marla was at home in our house. Mom and Aunt Della made this so for our families. It was not unusual for Marla to walk through the back door, into our kitchen, and immediately ask my mom if she could wash the dishes in the sink for her, the ones that had accumulated while keeping two boys fed throughout the day.

Together with my brother, we spent New Year's Eves at our home, being watched by Aunt Nellie and Uncle Clarence, as our parents went out to celebrate the coming of the New Year. When I started to drive, Marla and I took many, many trips to the local Dairy Queen. Once we took a wintry drive to the neighboring town of Indiana to buy something that is now long forgotten, only to have the battery in my parents' car give out as a blizzard started swirling around us. My dad and Uncle Mario drove through that blizzard to jump the battery for us.

Although living only a few blocks from each other, Marla and I rode different buses when we reached junior high. I sat, those junior high years, behind the bus driver with my friend since kindergarten, Garry, and with Alex, who was a fellow saxophone student. Yes, the three of us were small enough to sit three across in a bus seat.

When senior high started, Marla and I rode the same bus. Marla always got on one stop before me. She sat behind the bus driver, and as I boarded, I always sat next to her. Our conversations in the mornings covered mostly family activities, preparations for holidays, my brother, her sister, school stuff, and so on. We always began, though, with a recap of what our moms made for dinner the prior night.

I had countless dinners at Marla's, our families spent countless Christmases and Easters together, we ended many Thanksgivings at each other's homes, we made many trips to the Italian market in Greensburg, we sat with each other in church, and, well, the list goes on. I now try to call her every two weeks to stay in touch, a touch that is now separated by distance, but has always remained the same distance between my heart and hers.

***

Cousin Debbie was in the same grade as Chuckie, Marla, and I. Yes, four little Berninis, all with a good dose of Italian in them, all bonded by the same family values and ties, all in the same grade in the same school district. Debbie once said that if her family and Chuck's family hadn't moved to Ohio when we were ten years old, the four of us would have "ruled Blairsville High School."

Debbie was the fortunate one of us four Bernini cousins. She and her parents were the last Berninis to live in our grandma Bernini and Pap's home in Palmertown, Pennsylvania. Their home has such deep roots in our family that although it has new owners, it is still lovingly referred to as "the Palmertown House" when it is brought up in conversation. Debbie's parents moved in after my parents moved out, when Mom and Dad bought the two-story, yellow-clapboard house on Walnut Street. Debbie's parents remained there long enough for Debbie to acquire a strong mental picture of the interior of the house. Most importantly, she gained a strong mental picture of the kitchen, which for our Bernini family, was the heart of this home. Many stories still abound from times spent in that kitchen.

We four kids heard many, many stories about that home and our family who lived in it. Many of the stories still bring us to tears with laughter. But I must admit, for

Chuck, Marla, and me, we share a profound happiness for our cousin Debbie, in that she, out of the four of us, got to experience that home. And I think, too, we share a little envy because we didn't.

Debbie and her family moved to Ohio for her dad's career with General Motors when we were all about ten years old. Chuck's family moved to Ohio the same year for his parents to be closer to two of their daughters, whose lives and families were then centered there. These moves occurred when Chuck, Marla, Debbie, and I were all about to converge in Blairsville Junior High School as we entered the sixth grade.

During that time, the kids attending Burrell Elementary School were bused to Blairsville Junior High School to join the Blairsville Third Ward Elementary School kids in sixth grade. It was a big deal for all of us back then. Chuck, Marla, and I were Burrell kids. Cousin Debbie and her family lived in Blairsville, so she was a Third Ward kid. The possibilities for us as four cousins, supportive cousins, may have been endless had it not been for the moves when we were ten. As with Chuck and me, I am sure we all would have been a little competitive with each other…and a lot protective. And with our Bernini values, I believe we would, again, have had a mutual respect for our accomplishments as we all worked hard to achieve our grades…together.

I remember when Debbie's family moved. Mom and Dad took me to their home one evening before the moving company arrived. Packing was well underway. Debbie's dad offered my parents a set of twin beds that they could not take with them. My parents accepted the offer; they replaced the bunk beds that my little brother and I shared, an arrangement that never seemed to work for us. I think it had something to do with the required extra effort for Mom to change the bedding on the top bunk.

I had just started Cub Scouts. During this same evening, Debbie's mom offered me the Cub Scout uniform of Debbie's younger brother, Tommy. I recently mentioned this to Debbie. She stated that it was hard to believe that I could fit at that age into Tommy's Cub Scout uniform; he was such a little guy. Well, I could...and Tommy was younger than I.

As an epilogue to my Cub Scout career, I was asked to leave my Cub Scout pack by my den mother after my constructive criticism was considered by her to be more criticism than constructive. I remember walking out the screen door of her front porch, past my best friend, Joey, and the rest of my troop, my head erect, my dignity still intact. I only had my uncle Bob, the husband of my other aunt Helen, with whom to explain my supposed altercation with my former den mother. Uncle Bob was the district leader of all the area Cub Scout troops, and I was one of his favorite nephews—a favorite nephew now banished from a Cub Scout troop that he oversaw.

When I started sixth grade, I had a great crush on Wendy, one of my classmates. She was a Third Ward girl like my cousin Debbie. As Wendy and I were talking one day, I learned that she and my cousin Debbie were friends. I felt a void in my being when Wendy mentioned my cousin Debbie to me, my cousin Debbie who was now living in Ohio.

And then there was Debbie, the daughter of my childhood doctor—she, too, was a childhood friend of my cousin Debbie. And then in a recent text from my childhood sweetheart, Nancy, I discovered that she, too, knew my cousin Debbie...describing her "quick smile and cute, chiseled bob haircut" from their grade school days together, and going on to say she was "always joyful and I loved being around her." I must admit, she is still that way, Nancy.

Despite distance and time, Debbie and I are in touch and text frequently. There are some lost years we weathered, but the gap in time doesn't seem that long. The same with Chuck, as he now lives in Florida. But we four cousins have a supportive bond that still connects us.

How lucky for us.

***

The raw emotions of youth we once shared have been tempered with reason, tempered by experience, tempered with understanding and time. I am not sure how the day would have turned out for Mr. Coup if Debbie, Marla, and I had all been in that room together the day our cousin Chuckie was struck repeatedly by a twelve-inch wooden ruler. Perhaps the Italian side of us, then a force of four young, Italian cousins—*famiglia*—would have reacted differently. Back then, we all knew "family is family" and "you don't mess with family."

Famiglia.

Yes, how lucky for us.

White Christmases

I miss Christmas as a kid. The Christmases when I was under ten years old. They were the Christmases that came after we moved into our red-brick, ranch-style home in Edgemont. I was six when we moved. My brother was a newborn.

Christmas didn't start in August back then. There were no Black Fridays, Black Friday deals, or doorbusters starting in October, no Christmas catalogs with overly ornamented trees and uber decorations arriving in the mail in August, no Cyber Mondays, no knit hats with reindeer antlers on them, no ugly sweaters or Santa crawls, which seem to mock the meaning of this holiday. Christmas really didn't start until after Thanksgiving—the holiday that is a shadow of its former self, now glossed over by football on a day intended for family gatherings for meals, slowly consumed during long conversations, laughter, and reminiscing, wide-eyed kids at the tables, moms in aprons, dads carving turkeys and asking, "Who wants a drumstick?" and the traditional breaking of the wishbone. And of course, giving thanks in prayer as a family while gathered around a Thanksgiving table.

Back then, Thanksgiving ushered in the holiday season, a time of family, visiting, and sharing of meals and friendships. Anticipation would begin to build throughout the upcoming weeks, heralding a wonderful event that was more internal than external.

I walked to and from my elementary school back then. It was safe to do this. The lead-in to Thanksgiving was always the first Thanksgiving in Plymouth. There was no controversary about it back then. We were simply taught that people of different backgrounds gathered, gave thanks, and shared a meal together. Yes, people of different backgrounds, very different backgrounds and beliefs, who looked and dressed differently. The meaning we were taught of this event was of the sharing with others unlike ourselves for their support in very dire times, and giving thanks with and for them.

There were always Thanksgiving assemblies in our school lunchroom, which converted into an auditorium. Without fail, they included a stage full of kids on risers singing "Let There Be Peace on Earth" or "For the Beauty of the Earth." There is something magically innocent and angelic about a chorus of young children singing these songs; the lyrics, as delivered by the young voices of a new generation, carry a message of hope that transcends their telluric, secular meaning. The assemblies would end with a requisite, rousing rendition of "Over the River and Through the Woods." This song stayed with me as I alternated between humming it and singing it while walking home from school on the day before Thanksgiving. School always ended early the day before Thanksgiving.

I remember walking home that day, usually under soft-grey, clouded skies from which snow was gently falling.

Sometimes we already had a light, white ground cover. The snow was the signal that Christmas was around the corner. So was the arrival of the Sears Christmas catalog. Coming through the back door and into the kitchen of our home, never forgetting to remove my boots before entering the house, I would drop my book bag and start to peel off my gloves, scarf, hat, and coat, in that order.

I can still see Mom in the kitchen, in her blue-flowered apron that Grandma Olson made for her, with several newly baked pumpkin pies and her raisin-filled cookies cooling, their aromas enveloping her and now me. When old enough, my younger brother would be sitting on the kitchen floor next to Mom, playing with his red-rubber motorcycle with its yellow wheels.

The next day, we watched the Macy's Thanksgiving Day Parade with Dad in our living room. It wasn't a big commercial and celebrity event back then. Mom was in the kitchen preparing our Thanksgiving dinner while we were glued to the television. When younger, my brother sat on Dad's lap during the parade. When older, Bobby and I sat on the living room floor, waiting excitedly for Santa to appear at the end of Macy's parade. Bobby still played with his red-rubber motorcycle with the yellow wheels while watching.

Dad always had us pumped up for Santa's imminent appearance. If I had wandered into the kitchen to check on Mom's progress near to the time that Santa was going to make his appearance, Dad would yell, "Hey, Rodney! Get in here! Santa's coming!" I'd scamper back into the living room.

Dinner was usually in the early afternoon. The pumpkin pie with whipped cream came later. Supper was reheated mashed potatoes, sweet potatoes, stuffing, a slice of white meat, all smothered in turkey gravy. There was a little of Mom's homemade cranberry sauce, which I loved. And then, more pie. And cookies. Always cookies.

The next day, Christmas would begin for us. We decorated our tree that day, an event in which, annually, Dad called Mom into the living room to check that the tree was straight. "A little to the left. Too much, Bill! Take it to the right just a little." In our previous home on Walnut Street, we had live trees decorated with Grandma and Pap Bernini's brilliant-green Shiny-Brite ornaments with white flocking. But in the Edgemont house, we always had an artificial tree. Early on, it was an aluminum tree with blue teardrop ornaments, highlighted by a light wheel of rotating colors. Later, it was an artificial green tree with the same blue ornaments, but now complemented with silver garland and white lights. Regardless where we lived, we always decorated on that day. I still do.

Sometimes, though, on a warmer-weather Saturday in November, prior to Thanksgiving, Dad would carry the boxes of outdoor lights down from the attic, and the outdoor decorating commenced to avoid a later colder day for this annual event. I remember putting the lights up during a snowfall one winter. Brutal.

This was the ritual: At the end of each season, Dad always removed the bulbs before storing the strands of lights, placing the bulbs in a box separate from their wires. So before putting the lights back up, he had to test the light strings to ensure they still worked. Then, Dad hauled the ladder from the garage, climbed it, and with the aid of his trusty staple gun, began stringing the wires devoid of light bulbs around the entire perimeter of the eaves of our roofline. Once completed, my job was to hand Dad the lights to screw into the empty sockets.

Once or twice, he outlined our house in all blue lights, Dad's favorite decorative look. But we mostly used multicolored lights. My job was to hand Dad the lights—in order—white, yellow, orange, red, green, blue, repeat. I could not hold the lights while wearing my mittens, so I stuffed my mittens into the pockets of my winter jacket and began my duties. Dad got used to—no, expected—midway through the process for me to say, "Dad, my hands are cold," and a little later, "Dad, my hands are freezing!"

This was followed by, "Okay. We'll stop and go into the house until your hands are warm. Five minutes, okay?" He did mean "five minutes."

Mom was inside the house, arranging on the dining room table her hand-embroidered red Christmas tablecloth that her sister Nellie made for her. Mom liked fresh pine arrangements on the table. For good luck, we always burned a bayberry candle on Christmas Day, another on New Year's Day. We also had other sculpted candles of choirboys, a Christmas tree, and, of course, Santa. These were never lit.

Sometimes I was permitted to lay sheets of flocked, glittered cotton on our coffee table and make a Christmas village arrangement with cardboard houses and a cardboard church. The houses and church had colored-cellophane windows and were glittered, as if they had been adorned by a newly fallen snow. They also had holes in the back of them in which to insert lights. We never inserted lights. The coffee table had a cobalt-blue glass top. I separated the cotton to allow the cobalt-blue glass to show through as if the cobalt-colored glass were a pond next to the houses. And I had a multitude of green-plastic pine trees for my village. Each sat on a red round base; the green-plastic branches were attached to their wire trunks. They, too, were flocked with glitter "snow." Glitter was usually around the living room for months after the decorations were taken down.

Our Nativity crèche came when I was thirteen years old. Dad assumed the role each year of retrieving the box from the bedroom-closet shelf on which it was stored after each Christmas. He laid a blanket of more glittered cotton on the top of our television, then carefully and strategically arranged the scene of Baby Jesus in His manger, Mary, Joseph, the Wise Men, shepherds, and animals. Then he inserted a special light, representing the Star of Bethlehem, behind the angel atop the stable. Christmas for us was about the Nativity. This display represented all that Christmas meant to my family. The rest of the decorations and ensuing gifts played supporting roles.

We were never overdecorated. Nobody was. Most homes were decorated just enough to look festive. Slowly over the next week or so, other neighborhood homes would begin to sparkle with their own outdoor lights, Christmas trees displayed in windows, and fresh pine wreaths hung on doors.

And then we waited. School resumed on the Tuesday after Thanksgiving; Monday was a vacation day since it was the first day of deer season in Pennsylvania. Eventually, another school assembly was held by another class of girls and boys on risers, now singing religious and secular Christmas songs. Classrooms were decorated with garland chains of multicolored construction paper made by the young hands of their students; classroom bulletin boards took on a festive Christmas theme made of more construction paper, courtesy of the creative talents of our teachers. We all counted down the days while daydreaming in class of hoped-for toys, family gatherings, and that wonderful time off from school between Christmas and New Year's Day.

Families visited family members and friends before Christmas to admire their Christmas trees and the beautifully wrapped gifts beneath them. There was always a cookie tray—all homemade, of course—wherever we visited. Uncle Mario served Riunite in small juice glasses, an Italian way of serving wine, when we visited. I looked forward to our visit with our neighbors Elee and Joe; Elee made the best vanilla and anise pizzelles each year. We always dressed nicely for these visits. After Christmas, the visits were repeated, but now Santa had come and gone, and there were gifts to open. The cookie trays were still filled and generously offered.

Aunt Della and Uncle Mario hosted Christmas Eve dinner—one of two main annual dinners in an Italian household. The other is Easter. Mom was busy all day beforehand, preparing something to complement Aunt Della's menu. She covered whatever it was in aluminum foil and gingerly placed it on the seat of our car before we departed for Aunt Della and Uncle Mario's for Christmas Eve dinner. Mom always took an apron with her to help her sister Del.

There were kisses when we arrived and big embraces, sparkling eyes and wide smiles as if we hadn't seen each other in ages, despite Aunt Della and Uncle Mario only living a few blocks from our home. I can still see Aunt Nellie and Uncle Clarence arriving, Aunt Nellie in her red-cashmere swing coat and Uncle Clarence sporting his handsome fedora. More smiles, more hugs, more kisses all around as Aunt Nellie gingerly carried in her own homemade contribution for the dinner, also covered in aluminum foil. She always paused at the door to remove her winter boots with the fur trim and change into her high heels like those her sisters were wearing. Everyone was dressed up for this holiday family dinner.

Before dinner, there was always a little singing of Christmas songs led by Uncle Mario's tenor voice. He would eventually grab Aunt Della, taking her from her kitchen work, and swing her around to start dancing while singing a jolly Christmas song or an Italian love song. This was soon repeated with Mom and Aunt Nellie.

The ladies always smiled and laughed with an "Oh, Mario!" Aunt Della would exclaim, "Mario! I need to put dinner on the table!" but from her smiles and embrace, we all could tell she was enjoying a quick kitchen dance with her husband.

And Uncle Mario always ended his singing with a rousing "Santa Claus Is Coming to Town" for us kids. When he'd get to the line about being bad or good, Marla was always quick to say, "Daddy, I've been good!" As for me, I wasn't so quick to chime in, as I took mental inventory of the past year's…let's call them "events"…to access my qualifications.

Dinner was a multicourse feast that started with Cousin Marla saying grace, followed by all of us blessing ourselves. Then came course one: ravioli in broth. I loved them, but was always warned not to eat too many as this was only the first course. *Baccala*, or bacalao, came next. Uncle Mario had begun the soaking process one week prior to remove the salt used to cure it. It was served with *pasta nuzzi*, a homemade Italian noodle dish smothered in a walnut-and-cheese sauce. And then came the turkey with sweet potatoes, mashed potatoes, stuffing, and gravy. Aunt Della always served the turkey, and while carrying it to the table, she would jokingly say, "I made this for the Americans in the family." There was only one full non-Italian at the table then: my dad.

Aunt Della, Mom, and Aunt Nellie did all the serving. Aunt Della's holiday table, as she and her sisters were taught by their mother, my grandma Bernini, was always exquisitely set with her china, crystal, and flatware, all displayed on her holiday-themed linen tablecloth, which was complemented by matching linen napkins.

Sometime during dinner, Uncle Mario would call Marla and me over to his chair and offer us a little of his wine. We were told it was good for us, good for our blood. I'm not sure, today, if this was to accustom us to red wine as

Italian kids, or if he was really concerned about my childhood anemia of years past.

Two hours later, after many laughs and talk of "the
old days," dinner was over. Aunt Della, Mom, and Aunt
Nellie would then clear the table, and when that was complete, Aunt Della brought to the table her enormous tray
of Christmas cookies. Yes, all homemade. Yes, we were all
stuffed from dinner. Yes, we ate the cookies.

Around nine, we would retire to Aunt Della and Uncle
Mario's formal living room. People didn't sit in family
rooms back then during family gatherings such as this.
There were always compliments about their Christmas
tree and decorations. The adults talked; we kids sat and
listened while eyeing the gifts under their tree. My brother's name and mine were on several of them

All conversation stopped, though, at eleven when Uncle
Mario turned the television on, and we all watched the
WJAC news out of Johnstown. This station tracked the
progress of Santa and his reindeers over the state of Penn-
sylvania. Marla, Bobby, and I had our eyes glued to where
Santa and his reindeer were located. This was followed
soon by my dad saying, "Come on, we need to go home.
Santa's on his way, and you two need to go to bed."

The magic of Santa was over for me when I was about
eight years old, but the thrill of Santa remained with me
as I experienced it through the eyes and excitement of my
younger brother. The Christmas Eve celebrations evolved as
we grew older. Midnight Mass replaced tracking Santa and
"going to bed." The family dinners continued unchanged.

So did the hugs, kisses, trays of cookies, and, most importantly, the unspoken but deeply felt family love.

For many years, as we departed Aunt Della and Uncle Mario's home, either after tracking Santa or when leaving for Midnight Mass, we departed amid a blanket of freshly fallen, beautiful white snow covering their yard. Sometimes snowflakes were still lightly falling. The outdoor lights of Aunt Della and Uncle Mario's back porch illuminated their glistening snow-covered yard on those dark, crisp, cold nights, allowing us to appreciate for just a moment, the gentle, silent, serene beauty of it all.

Yes, the gentle, silent, serene beauty of a white Christmas Eve.

Yes, I miss Christmases as a kid.

Midnight Mass

I just watched an incredible Christmas concert given by the main choir and the gospel choir of Marble Collegiate Church in New York City. For those who may remember, it is the church once headed by Norman Vincent Peale. I am sure most of our mothers, the mothers of us Baby Boomers, read his signature book, *The Power of Positive Thinking*. The main choir performed Handel's "For Unto Us a Child Is Born" from his *Messiah*. It was powerful. And meaningful. And moving. The concert ended with "Joy to the World."

I found my memories going back to Saint Francis Church in Graceton, Pennsylvania. I was about twelve or thirteen years old, maybe slightly younger. My family departed Aunt Della and Uncle Mario's home, where we just had our traditional Christmas Eve dinner, an Italian feast of legendary proportions. Their car followed our car to Saint Francis for Midnight Mass. We arrived a little before eleven. The parking lot was already full.

We sat in the back right side of the church. By then, the church itself was almost full. Aunt Nellie and Uncle Clarence were a few pews behind us. I am sure Aunt Marian and Uncle Reno were there, too, with Louie and Diana, who may have been married to Bill then; they always sat on the left side of the main aisle of Saint Francis. Cousin

Betty Lou and her family may have been in church then, too. There was always something comforting about all my Bernini relatives being in church together—the smiles; the waves; Betty Lou's big, playful grin as she turned her head to survey the congregation to see if we had arrived.

The church was beautifully decorated as always. The creche was magnificent; the trees flanking the altar were beautiful. Mass started with Father Kowal serving his congregation once again, that night surrounded by his numerous altar boys in their red cassocks and white surplices. Louie was once an altar boy and may have served Midnight Mass. By now, I am sure he had completed his altar-boy service. Betty Lou's sons, Chris and Greg, were altar boys, too. So were my brother and I. Chris was probably serving that night. It was a Bernini tradition for most of us boys.

The church dimmed for "Silent Night." Always moving, always powerful, always a few tears here and there as the song penetrated souls while the glow of the altar candles spread a warmth, a feeling of communion, over the congregation. There was standing room only by the time Midnight Mass began.

Aunt Della and Mom usually sat together at my hometown church of Saint Bonaventure each Sunday. They placed Cousin Marla and me next to each other, where we would sing our hearts out. Marla always remembered all the lyrics to all the hymns.

At this Midnight Mass, Mom and Aunt Della sat next to each other. When the last song, "Joy to the World," began, Mom, a soprano, and Aunt Della, an alto, blended their sisterly voices perfectly. Uncle Mario's tenor was strong. The entire church was singing. Loud, clear, and joyous. Exuberant.

We departed with many warm family hugs and kisses, hearty "Merry Christmases," and, of course, meaningful "*Buon Natales.*"

I remember this night well. Like yesterday.

Progress

I love winter. I always did. I believe I am in a minority with this love. For me, it echoes a magical time in my childhood home in Edgemont, a suburb of my hometown of Black Lick. The first snow turned our lovely little suburb into a true winter wonderland for me. The pure virgin snow laid a blanket of white across the yards, making everything look clean and bright. And peaceful. Suddenly the greys of winter sparkled.

From our dining room window, an early morning snow of a few inches connected all the yards—those of Elee and Joe, Helen and Dick, Nancy and Joe, through to the upsloped yard of Joni's family. A seamless, undulating, gentle covering of pristine, glittering white creating a oneness that was perhaps seen and felt by all the neighbors back then, connecting us in yet another way. The yards did not have fences, except for the one needed by Nancy and Joe for little Susie, but even it seemed to disappear into the blanket of white. If the snow was still gently falling, the millions of unique flakes brought a soft veil to the scene.

From the large picture window in our living room, we looked across the road to Mr. and Mrs. Gorton's Dutch Colonial home. To its right was a deliberately prominent stone chimney that climbed the side of the house, perfect for Santa's reindeer to scale on Christmas Eve. To the left of their home was the stone fountain, which Mr. Gorton sculpted, cascading water into his koi pond, now frozen over by the winter's cold. Their home was painted seafoam green; a white aluminum awning shadowed the entire sweeping front porch that ran the full length of the house, framed by a multitude of rhododendrons in front of it. The seafoam green, the whiteness of the awning, the grand chimney, the stonework of the fountain, and the rhododendrons in their winter hibernation—they all had their beauty enhanced by the unbroken blanket of snow. And beyond the Gorton's home was the majestic hillside of Grafton, again covered in an unbroken white that was pierced by evergreens and now-naked deciduous trees.

Yes, I love the snow. And for some reason, while peering out our windows, sometimes with Mom or my younger brother next to me, our home felt a little warmer, a little cozier, a little more enveloping.

It's all gone now.

I wish I could say this all belonged to another young family, but it doesn't.

Soon after my parents built our 1960s ranch-style home in Edgemont, I overheard them talking about rumors that the state of Pennsylvania planned to widen into a four-lane highway the road in front of our new home. I was six years old and too young to understand the impact of this possibility on the just-completed achievement of designing and participating in the construction of our home, a home for which Mom designed her own kitchen and Dad and Uncle

Pete personally varnished all the oak floors, doors, trim, and cabinets. A home in which my parents had sunk their life's savings.

But the rumors came and went over the next thirty years or so, like a recurring thief lurking in the shadows of speculation, ready to take away the security of a home my parents made for themselves and their two growing sons. It put a pall over our home and frequently reared its head. As children of the Great Depression—and, later, participants in what made the Greatest Generation great—the security and achievement of home ownership was not only a goal; it represented a very deep personal success story of survival and pride. Not pride in the sense of "proud," but rather "satisfaction" in the results of their own collaborative achievement as a young couple of their generation.

In the early 1970s, nearby farmland was sold to begin construction of an electricity-generating power plant. It was to be fueled by the abundant underground veins of bituminous coal in the area. Coal mines had been a source of employment and wealth for the surrounding communities since the mid-1800s. Indeed, my grandfather Bernini—Pap to us—emigrated from his hometown of Solignano, Italy, to this area to seek his fortune, his bride, and to raise his family with money made from employment in the mines. His four sons all entered the mines at the age of fourteen, when boys could be employed to mine the coal veins that were in areas too constricted for grown men to squeeze their bodies into. Later, one of these sons, Carlo, whom we affectionately called Uncle Keck, went on to own five of the local coal mines.

As a teenager, I watched from our home as the power plant took shape on a nearby hill overlooking the towns of Coral and Graceton. Eventually, two smokestacks started to emerge above the trees lining the top of the hill. Later, a wide, circular cooling tower of cement peaked above the trees, and then another cooling tower next to it. The power plant brought the promise of increased employment opportunities and tax monies for the neighboring towns and schools.

It succeeded in all these promises.

And with it came increased truck traffic in front of our home and on the farmland roads of Grafton. Grafton was the former farm of Sumner Graff. Sumner was the son of John Graff, a merchant and a pillar in the local arm of the Underground Railroad, which helped slaves reach their freedom. Sumner, who served on the board of directors of the Black Lick Bank in the late 1800s, provided a large section of his farm on which to build the suburb of Grafton. Sumner, too, was the great-great-uncle of a later John Graff, the John Graff who became the husband of my dad's sister Ruth. My cousin Barb likes to reminisce about the time on her family's farm when she spent summers with her grandparents, often leisurely basking in the quiet of farm mornings, fresh eggs for breakfast, and waking to crisp, cool, clean breezes wafting through bedroom windows, all prior to those mornings being pierced by the rumbling and shifting of gears of large trucks hauling coal to the power plant.

The power plant was finally declared operational, and then one day we saw steam rising from the cooling towers.

A large white plume, then two white plumes hovered over the distance hilltop like fluffy white clouds, later disappearing into the atmosphere. At the same time, and perhaps coincidentally, neighborhoods started finding a fine film of white powder on their porches and cars each morning. Mom could often be found on summer mornings wiping the filmy, greasy residue from the outdoor furniture on our back porch.

Soon, a formal announcement from the state of Pennsylvania was issued, which, for my parents, chillingly stated that a larger access road to the power plant was needed for the increasing number of trucks carrying coal to it. Three alternate routes were offered during a series of community and town-hall meetings that were held over the next several years. One option put the road right through Edgemont, right through my parents' living room.

***

This was not the first time in the twentieth century that my hometown of Black Lick was the recipient of decisions such as this, decisions which required sacrificing the livelihood and homes of its residents in the name of progress. Why a direct impact on the actual town itself of Black Lick? To this day, I cannot understand why.

As a child of the town, to me the impacts felt more like assaults. This was the third major impact inflicted on this wonderful little town of people who had truly formed a community of love, support, civic pride, and genuinely embraced goals and aspirations that form the basis of human existence The town had a "Jimmy Stewart movie" quality about it, a Bedford Falls quality from *It's a Wonderful Life*. It was a town that truly loved and supported its neighbors.

At the turn of the last century, Black Lick was a thriving industrial town nestled in the heart of the picturesque Allegheny Mountains of Western Pennsylvania. It had its own train station and was an important stop between the towns of Blairsville and Indiana, where, by the way, Jimmy Stewart was born and raised. The Josephine Furnace and Coke Company supplied coke to the steel mills of Pittsburgh from what seemed to be an unlimited supply of nearby coal. The Marshall Foundry was making ingot molds for the production of steel, the owners of which built the suburb of Marshall Heights for their executives and employees. Other local industries at this time included the Enameling Works; the Glass Works; the E. A. Schooly Torpedo works, which, yes, made torpedoes; the S. J. Sides Lumber Company, which cut railroad and mine ties; and the Elite Printing Company of A. M. Barrow, which eventually became the Commercial Printing Company.

Main Street had a trolley, a requisite of its day. The Nehrig (later Bernini) Hotel provided meals and lodging for the businessmen and women who traveled to Black Lick from Pittsburgh and other out-of-town locations and for the performers at the Palmer Opera House, one of the first-class theaters for opera and touring companies in the county in which Black Lick was located. Lining Main Street, there were numerous grocery and dry goods stores, notions stores, confectionaries and restaurants, a clothing store, and Schrom's Pharmacy. Women could buy fabrics, threads, and yarns at the Singer Sewing Store, and men could have a daily shoeshine in shops such as the one operated by Mentore Dallara, another Italian immigrant.

There were seven suburbs: Palmertown, Marshall Heights, Grafton, Edgemont, Bell's Mill, Campbell's Mill, and Josephine, which itself was once a town, but was absorbed into Black Lick. Most of the suburbs of Black Lick had their own schools providing education up to the eighth grade. Five houses of worship echoed the diversity of the population of Italians, Czechs, Poles, Slavs, Germans, Syrians, and others, all of whom lived side by side, intermarried, and raised families to support the next generation of the town. And Black Lick had its own bank and its own undertaker.

And, unfortunately, as was often the case back then, as it is now, the town also had its own small, but psychologically powerful, anti-immigrant group of people who burned crosses on Grafton Hill to remind the Catholics, Italians, Poles, and others who formed the heart of the town, and its base of success through their work in the local industries and mines, of their perceived place in society.

The residents of Black Lick, its industrial base, and the rich veins of coal under the town and surrounding areas supported each other in a mutually beneficial, symbiotic relationship, though. Businesses begetting businesses, employment begetting employment, generations begetting generations.

But through the 1920s and 1930s, many of the industrial-based companies were purchased, in the name of progress, by larger companies that, ignoring the large population base of skilled, knowledgeable workers, moved their operations elsewhere, gutting the town of a large share of its employment and revenues. The coal that was all mined locally and supported many of these businesses was now being trucked miles away to support these companies in their new locations.

The devastating Johnstown Flood of 1936—the second such devastating flood to hit Johnstown in the span of forty years—resulted in the recognized need for a flood-control plan to spare this nearby city noted for its steel production. The solution adopted by the state of Pennsylvania was to build the Conemaugh Dam. The dam required an area of overflow runoff. The selected area: one-half of the populus and vibrant town of Black Lick. So half the town was leveled, its residents displaced, and businesses closed to mitigate the probable future flooding of Johnstown.

And now, a decision was made to run a four-lane highway through another section of the town.

***

By this time, the flood-control project had turned what was left of Black Lick into a bedroom community supported by a few resilient local businesses. But, more importantly, the town was supported by a strong, well-educated, civic-minded foundation of leadership that crossed nationalities, education levels, and areas of expertise. All patriots of World War II who knew how to challenge and challenge hard, how to fight and fight hard. I know. My mom and dad were part of that foundation.

I attended a town-hall meeting with Mom and Dad when I visited for several days. I was about forty years old at the time. Representatives from the state of Pennsylvania were present, replete with a plethora of glossy charts, pointers, and smooth-talking speakers in suits and blazers. The meeting was held in the auditorium of Burrell Elementary School. The room was brimming over with townspeople and press. The presenters touted why the citizens of Black Lick should feel proud of sacrificing their lifelong homes and businesses in the name of progress to build a road through their neighborhood, through their town, which had already been severely impacted by previous decisions such as this one.

During the meeting, I questioned one of the representatives, asking him to explain how taking away the homes of residents—many of whom were entering their retirement years and looking forward to sitting back and enjoying the fruits of a lifetime of their labors, having built a life of security centered on their homes, the mortgages of which were ghosts of a distant past—could be seen as a positive action in the name of progress.

The gentleman in his brown-and-ivory plaid blazer explained to me, in a very "son, you need to understand" manner, that he understood my concern. In fact, he went on to say that he had to displace his own mother from her home to build a road and that she was now doing fine living in a retirement home.

I felt a sense of futility at that moment.

I guess the actuarial tables for this project had indicated that the community pushback would only be temporary.

My brother told me later that of the three alternate routes presented at these successive series of town-hall meetings, one was rejected due to the farmland that would be consumed by the road. The second was rejected due to the habitat of a species of endangered rodents that would be affected. Yes, you read that right. The only option, therefore, was to run the road through the living room of my parents' home and through the homes of their numerous neighbors who lived along the route that became the finalist.

Dad passed in 1999 at the age of seventy-six. My brother and I still wonder if the effort and stress to save his lifelong hometown, combined with the stress of losing his home, the home into which he had poured thirty-seven years—half his life—contributed to his early demise.

***

One year later, Mom received official notice from the state of Pennsylvania that the road was approved and construction would begin. The state of Pennsylvania offered to buy her home and demolish it to make way for the road. The offer wasn't enough to replace the home, either by building from scratch or buying another.

The industriousness of my brother, coupled with his dogged determination when he sets his mind on something, led to a decision to simply move our home. He found a half-acre lot in Edgemont—set on a gently sloping hill away from the impending construction, in a field where corn once grew—in an area that had been divided into lots for new-home construction. The lot he chose was next to the new Greek Orthodox church. My brother found a company in New England that moved lighthouses and contracted them to bring their expertise and rigs to Black Lick to relocate our childhood home and, hopefully, provide Mom with continuity and peace in the home she had known since my brother was born, now thirty-nine years prior.

I was there on the day of the move. When I arrived, the house was jacked up on support beams, and a wheeled chassis had been constructed under it. Beneath the chassis, I could see the remnants of our 1960s basement turned family room. Mom had been staying with her sister Della. She arrived in tears.

For our peaceful neighborhood, this represented the first sign that their lives were being interrupted; going forward, nothing would ever be the same.

I had been at our home several weeks prior to help Mom, my brother, his wife, and our relatives pack the house for the move. We were told that the contents of the house could remain inside it; the weight of the house would prevent any movement of its contents during the actual move. Nonetheless, we emptied the cabinets and closets into boxes and covered everything in blankets and sheets. Furniture was moved against the walls, just in case.

I did not want to leave behind the remains of our two black toy poodles, Gigi I and Gigi II. They were buried next to the garage. They were so much a part of our lives;

they needed to move with the house. We loved them like daughters and sisters. I did not want them to be excavated and paved over by construction equipment. Gigi II had been buried wrapped in her favorite handmade, quilted pink blanket. I was there when both were interred; it wasn't as if I didn't know where their remains were. I dug frantically to find them. I could find nothing. To this day, I live with regret that I could not find our dear sweet pups.

As for our three parakeets, hamster, white mice, and numerous fish, who were also buried next to the garage, I didn't look for them. They were all older than our Gigis. At one time, as kids, my brother and I made wooden tombstones for all of them. I was sure they were now the dust to which we all are destined to return.

When the home was pulled from our lot, I peered down into the basement. There lay the green carpet of our family room, still in place. Our pink furnace was on its side, severed from its piping, some of which was still attached to the furnace. Next to where the basement stairway had been lay the knotty-pine walls of the stairway, the knotty-pine walls that Dad loved so much. And next to the walls was the oak staircase, it too on its side, still intact, huddling next to the knotty-pine walls that it once supported, perhaps each giving comfort to the other on that brisk autumn day.

Mom wanted to walk next to her home as it was being moved to its new lot. I remember Mom reaching up to touch its elongated, textured, oxblood-colored bricks, the bricks she chose when it was built, as her home hovered above her on its chassis. She chose to wear one of

Dad's jackets that day, his red Lands' End jacket with the navy-fleece lining. My brother and I walked next to her. The local press was there for the story of our house being moved. A photo of Mom next to her jacked-up home going down Route 119 South appeared the next day in the local papers. The last time her photo had been in the papers was as a community leader negotiating the location of the road to avoid an event such as this.

The state of Pennsylvania built a noise-barrier wall where our backyard was once located. This was to prevent the remaining neighborhood of Edgemont from hearing the endless din of trucks passing by at all hours of the day and night. It stood where our summer barbecues and outdoor dinners with Elee and Joe were once held, where my brother once splashed as a toddler in his baby pool, where our Gigis frantically ran in their futile attempts to catch birds, where every year friends and relatives were amazed at Mom's spectacular flowers during the summer. When I pass it now, I think of our Gigis, our parakeets and fish.

For the neighborhood homes remaining, the beautiful snow-covered hill in Grafton punctuated with evergreens and naked deciduous trees in winters is no longer visible due the functional, grey-cement, nondescript noise barrier. Elee and Joe's living room windows now face that wall, a living room where each Christmas our family once celebrated with them, my brother and I enjoying Elee's amazing homemade cookies and pizzelles while the adults toasted with a holiday drink, all admiring their Christmas tree and peering out those windows to the sparkling, snow-covered hill in Grafton.

The beautiful expanse of neighborhood yards on a snowy morning is now broken...homes missing...and in their place, a wall.

The power plant has since ceased operations.

The now less-traveled road remains, though, as does the nondescript wall still blocking the serene, gentle beauty of a friendly, peaceful neighborhood on a snowy morning, a neighborhood that once was.

Progress.

Archangels

Yesterday was the Second Sunday of Lent. I was selected to be lector that day at the 8:00 a.m. Mass at the Chapel of the Sacred Hearts of Jesus and Mary. Virginia, the church administrator, provides the lectors with an annual study guide of the Sunday and holiday readings. The book covers the readings themselves, the history and meaning behind them, the pronunciations of the ancient names, and some suggestions on when and how to emphasize certain phrases and words. I study my readings every night before serving as lector.

The Gospel for the Second Sunday of Lent is always the Transfiguration of Jesus. God's pronouncement about Jesus in this Gospel, "This is my Beloved Son. Listen to Him," was, is, and will always be the power and lesson of this amazing event. The images many of us have of this event are well ingrained in our minds. For me, I can see the cloud in the sky from which the pronouncement came and the image of Jesus as he stood with Moses and Elijah on the mountain. As for Moses, his image is clear for me, but for Elijah, Peter, James, and John, I haven't been so clear as to how they may have looked in their lives.

As many across the globe, I have been watching the series *The Chosen* on the life of Jesus. The actor playing

Jesus has a striking resemblance to how Jesus has been portrayed throughout the centuries and to my image of Him. In the series, the Apostles who accompany Jesus to the mountain—Peter, James, and John—give a completely different perspective than how they have been portrayed in religious art. They are seen, live, and act as people we all could know in our daily lives, people we all could have befriended at some point. As Father Alex read the Transfiguration Gospel and I listened to his homily, I had a very different image of Peter, James, and John. I saw them as the actors from *The Chosen*: everyday people, just like you and me. And they were. But chosen for a very different role than any of us.

My first reading prior to the Gospel on this Sunday was on Abraham's sacrifice of his son Isaac. It is always a startling reading, as Abraham is asked by God to sacrifice his only son. But as we know, God then steps in and through his messenger, tells Abraham not to harm the boy in any way; then He promises Abraham that for his devotion to God, his offspring shall number as the stars in the sky. Considering that Abraham is the father of three great religions—Christian, Jewish, and Muslim—this promise was clearly fulfilled. An amazing gift to Abraham from an amazing God.

My second reading was from the letter of Saint Paul to the Romans (Romans 8:31b–34, New Catholic Bible). It begins with "If God is for us, who can be against us?" As I read this opening line, I paused between the words "us" and "who," then looked up at the congregation. I'll leave it at that.

After Mass, I did my usual lector post-Mass duties to assist Gerta in clearing the altar and the credence table, preparing the lector book for the next Mass, and checking the pews for bulletins and other articles left behind by the congregants. The wall on the south side of the Chapel encases floor-to-ceiling windows that look out onto the Chapel's landscaped courtyard and then out to the sidewalk of Thirty-Third Street in Manhattan. The gigantic windows allow natural light to pour into the Chapel during daylight hours, and at night, there is soft interior lighting. Both forms of light permit the beautiful artwork and architecture of the Chapel to be viewed by passersby on Thirty-Third Street.

As I was walking the center aisle during my pew-checking duties, I looked up. Through the gigantic windows, I saw a young man with dark, curly hair emerging from under a ski cap; he was walking up the steps leading into the courtyard from the sidewalk on Thirty-Third Street. He blessed himself as he entered the courtyard. He then stopped and, peering through the gigantic windows, fixed his gaze on me. He didn't move. I caught his gaze and nodded. His gaze remained fixed on me.

After my nod, I continued checking the pews and then met Gerta in the narthex outside the office door of the Chapel. The office door is adjacent to two large glass doors that serve as the entrance to the Chapel. We had started our usual post-Mass banter when Gerta looked up and commented on a homeless man in the courtyard. It was the young man with the ski cap and black, curly hair. Only now, he was looking at Gerta and me through the glass panes of the entrance doors. His gaze, once again, was fixed.

The young man approached the Chapel's glass doors, partially opened one, and squeezed through. As the door closed behind him, he blessed himself once again. Walking over to Gerta and me, he asked, "Is this a Catholic church?" After Gerta and I simultaneously acknowledged that it was, the young man blessed himself again.

His face was calm. His demeanor was calm. And although it was about eighteen degrees outside, his face didn't show any signs of the bitter early-morning cold. The young man told us he was Catholic. I said hello and invited him to stay a while in the sanctuary, as it would remain open for private devotion until the next Mass. He asked if Mass was taking place. Gerta explained that the next Mass was at noon. He was dressed in a navy-blue parka, black pants, and carried a cup of coffee from a local bodega in one hand and a backpack in the other.

There was nothing about him that seemed to indicate that he was not in his right mind or that he was looking for support as a homeless person. In fact, he seemed to have a sense of strength and direction about him. His face was a countenance that drew in both Gerta and me. If Caravaggio were still alive and painting, he could have used the young man as a model. And his manner of slow, deliberate speech seemed mesmerizing to both of us. The young man's absolute calmness slowed the frantic pace and clipped conversation that Gerta and I usually exchange as we rush to prepare the Chapel for the next Mass.

And there we were, the three of us, consciously looking at each other. Just looking. Time seemed to have stopped for that moment. For me, no thoughts were occurring as to who this young man was or what he wanted. I suspect Gerta felt the same. I glanced at her out of the corner of my eye, and her eyes were fixed on him too, her face now calm despite the pace of that morning's activities.

The young man asked my name. I told him. He asked Gerta her name. She told him. He extended his hand to shake mine and then did the same for Gerta. I watched his hand as he extended it to me, and as I took it, I looked up at him and realized that my "radar up," which is normal for many New Yorkers, did not signal danger. I sensed that Gerta felt the same.

The young man with dark, curly hair then said, "My name is Michael. Like the Archangel." He smiled slightly... the closed-mouth smile that comes when experiencing a pleasant moment of life. As he spoke, he looked intently at both of us.

The young man then asked for my phone number. I told him I could not give it to him. He then asked how he could remember where the church was when he returned. Gerta handed him the Sunday bulletin and pointed out the address of the Chapel on it. He read it, then took the bulletin and put it in his backpack.

After taking the bulletin, he lifted his backpack, turned, and walked toward the front door. Holding his coffee in one hand, he pushed the brass lever of the front door to exit with his other hand. The young man with the black, curly hair emerging from his ski cap then turned to look at us as he exited the front door. Looking over his shoulder, he said, "I've been a Catholic since birth."

Gerta replied that she was too. I said, "Me too. All my life." He then stood in the courtyard for a while, looking back through the glass panes of the entrance doors.

Gerta looked at me, and in her wonderful Austrian accent, asked, "What do you think just happened?"

I replied, "I don't know. Sometimes, Gerta, we just don't know in the moment."

When I departed, he was still there in the courtyard. I noticed that his gaze was fixed on me again as I walked out the door. I waved and said, "Have a nice Sunday."

He answered back, "Is today Sunday?"

I am reminded of Hebrews 13:2, which reads:

> *Let mutual love continue, and do not forget to offer hospitality to strangers, for by doing this, some have entertained angels without knowing it.*

He said his name was Michael. Like the Archangel.

Ozzy on the Doorstep

I received the following email from my brother:

Four weeks ago, Becky found two kittens only hours old in the grass at her mother's home in Pennsylvania. A mother cat had abandoned them. Both kittens were crying and there was a cold rain/snow storm on the way. Becky picked up both kittens and brought them into her mother's house. She bought kitten formula and began to feed them. She brought the kittens to our home and when I first saw them, they didn't even look like kittens. They were smaller than my palm. She had read that kittens had to be fed every two hours. She would feed them throughout the night and Zack would feed them during the day.

There was a baby girl and a baby boy. The girl was having trouble eating. Becky took them to the vet to have them checked out and was advised the little girl wasn't going to make it. We lost her. But we still have the boy. His name is Ozzy.

Becky continued to hand feed Ozzy using a syringe. It was fun to watch how eager he was to eat. The vet gave us two IV bags filled with saline solution that we had to microwave until warm. We made him his own little waterbed from the saline bags to keep him warm. He had to be kept at 86 degrees until he could regulate his own body temperature. Ozzy grew very quickly and now today he is walking on his own. We still need to make sure he gets to his litter box. He gives us a signal when he needs to go.

In only three weeks, he developed a personality. He doesn't know how to run yet. I walked in the door on Friday night and he did a speed walk down the hallway to me. He reminded me of Marvin the Martian with two sets of legs. He stalks and chases his shadow and likes to attack the gray spots on our speckled carpet. Becky has reduced his feeding now to every four hours.

He will not allow us to read our phones, books or use our computers because he must have attention.

None of this message surprised me. My brother always had a soft spot in his heart for animals. He inherited this from our mother. Mom once started feeding a stray cat that appeared on our back porch one summer. It was my duty, in addition to drying dishes and taking out the garbage, to take a small green ceramic bowl of leftovers out to this lonely little cat each night after dinner and place it next to our porch door. I then retrieved the empty green bowl for washing. Later, two cats appeared, waiting for Mom's dinner of leftovers that I delivered to them in the same small green ceramic bowl. Then there were three cats...

One night, Dad returned home from work, parked the car in the driveway, and as usual, entered the house through the door of the kitchen, where Mom was preparing dinner and I was sitting at the kitchen table.

"Vease," Dad said, "There are twenty cats on our back porch. You have got to stop feeding them."

Of course, my youthful boyhood curiosity took me out to the back porch. Sure enough, twenty or so cats...sitting on the porch and on the decorative red-brick half wall surrounding the porch, staring at me with tails swaying, probably looking at me in bewilderment as to why I didn't have their green ceramic bowl of leftovers at that moment.

I still wonder where all those cats had been hiding in our neighborhood. They certainly weren't visibly wandering around the neighborhood during daylight hours. In fact, I only remember one very beautiful brown tabby that roamed the neighborhood during those days. She was a gentle cat. I guess she had a lot of friends elsewhere.

I could not help but wonder, as I read my brother's message, how Ozzy and his sister ended up in the front yard of the home of my brother's mother-in-law. Bob sent a photo to me of Ozzy soon after Becky took Ozzy and his sister home with her. He was truly a newborn, lying in a curled position, eyes closed, and fitting snuggly into the palm of my brother's hand. Clearly his mother abandoned him at the doorstep, perhaps deliberately within a range that either my brother, his wife, or one of their children would see them. I believe this was intentional on the part of their mother cat.

But what happened to her? Was she ill and knew she could not raise them, so she scoured the neighborhood looking for kind souls who loved animals, as my brother and his family do? Perhaps she peered into the windows of the home of Becky's mother and saw her grandchildren and the weekend interactions of the family. Maybe she knew she couldn't support her newborns in the wild, scrounging for food at night in a suburban neighborhood of tightly sealed garbage cans and few other random food options. Or maybe she was simply transporting the newborns to a better location to keep them warm and in the process met her demise.

I prefer to believe that she knew she could not raise her kittens, and after thoroughly researching nearby homes by peering into windows, she realized the home of Becky's mother was best for her kittens. It looked like a good home, a home that would love her kittens.

She left them at the doorstep.

Abandonment could not have been an easy decision for the mother of Ozzy and his sister. As a mother, she was giving up a part of herself that she had carried within her for two months. She may have gently laid them in a noticeable location where they would be found, looked at them one last time, gently gave them a goodbye lick, maybe rested her motherly paw on them one last time, turned, and walked away as they were crying for her warmth and love. Perhaps she turned to look back, wondered for a moment if she was making the right decision, but then turned and walked away knowing she was, love tugging at her heart, tears in her eyes, a prayer in her mind.

I say this because I believe animals have souls.

We often read the heartbreaking stories of newborn babies being left on doorsteps. Little, helpless bundles of new life, innocent of all that is happening with their entry into the world. This was a practice that once was common, as parents were unable, for whatever reason, to care for their new children, or perhaps just wanted them to have the opportunity for a better life.

During the 1800s in England and elsewhere, babies were abandoned to orphanages, which at times led them to be raised to labor in "workhouses." In Ancient Rome, newborns were often thrown into the Tiber River. I had a reason to research these practices several years ago for a study I was doing. Each passage was a gut-wrenching read. I found the following in LegacyTree.com; it's about yet another practice in those days:

> The Catholic Church, concerned for the souls of these babies, played a large role in the development of foundling homes. To allow for the anonymity of the mother, and thus keep her and her family from being disgraced, the "ruota dei proietti" or "foundling wheel" was instituted.

The foundling wheel was a wooden, cylindrical box that was installed in the outer wall of a hospital, church, or in smaller communities, a midwife's home, into which a newborn could be placed. The wheel was then turned, so that the baby went inside, without anyone being able to see (from the inside) who placed the baby on the wheel. The person leaving the baby then pulled a bell that was near the wheel, notifying the attendant inside that a foundling had arrived.

Ozzy is another life saved. He is a kitten who, left at a doorstep, fell into the warmth, support, and kindness of a good home.

I am a firm believer that we are all on this earth to help one another. This extends to all living creatures, animals and plants alike. And I believe, if we recognize and act on this gift within ourselves, we can and should help each other.

And yes, plants. I once read that mature trees in forests will bend their top leafy branches to permit sunlight to fall upon the young saplings around the base of their trunks, giving the saplings the warmth and nurturing of the sun to assist in their growth.

My brother and I grew up with animals. There was my dog Fluffy who I had prior to my brother's birth. And Fluffy was followed by Gigi I and then Gigi II, both black toy poodles with big personalities, who were completely spoiled. We referred to them as our sisters. There were our white mice, our hamster (only one—it escaped its cage and scurried down the shower drain; Dad had to retrieve him with the vacuum), and our myriad fish. We also had our blue parakeet, Dickie Bird, who was a gift from my godparents, Aunt Nellie and Uncle Clarence. When he went to his next life, he was replaced by green and blue parakeets my brother and I named Rub and Scrub.

The owners of Gigi I had already named her when we adopted her. She was given the name Pepé le Pew Gigette. The Pepé le Pew part was from her father's AKC lineage. We simply called her Gigi. Gigi II was not named when we adopted her. She was about three years younger and had the same parents, so she was a sister of Gigi I. We decided, in the car on the way home with that little bundle of black fur, that we would name her Gigi Louise. Gigi after Aunt Giggi, my mom's oldest sister, and Louise after Mom's middle name. Her AKC name was Gigi Louise Olson.

The mother of both Gigis was not present when we selected them. The litters of both Gigis were cute, each a little bundle of squiggly puppies still not sure of their surroundings. I now wonder what Gigi I's mother felt when she returned to her litter to find her baby Gigette not there. There had to be a sense of alarm—"Where's my Gigette?!?!"—a second counting of the pups around her, and perhaps a frantic search followed. The realization that little Gigette wasn't there had to be surreal for her. Eventually, this may have been followed by an acceptance of her loss, a loss that never goes away.

My ten-year-old mind wasn't thinking in those terms then. We had a new puppy, and that was my focus.

A similar situation must have occurred when we took Gigi II from this same mother. I wonder if she ever grew accustomed to having her babies taken from her. Did she ever suspect that when she was lifted from her bed, surrounded by her babies, "Oh no! It's happening again."? Then, one day, returning to her bed to find all the new pups gone.

Both Gigis, I will admit, found a very good home with my family. They had their special handmade quilted blankets, baby dolls, and plush toys (not squeaky toys), a beautiful wicker bed and special pillow, my brother and me to lie against while napping on the sofa, special meals of boiled chicken and sometimes grilled steak, a great yard in which to chase birds, and my mother's and dad's legs to sit against when visitors called. Both hated paperboys and trips to the vet, but liked to rummage through Aunt Della's open handbag for gum, which they loved to chew. And then there was the excessive attention they received whenever Aunt Della, Uncle Mario and Marla, or Aunt Nellie and Uncle Clarence came through the kitchen door to visit. Aunt Della often grabbed their front legs and danced with them.

And so, this was the type of home in which we were taught to raise and nurture our pets. I am sure it is the type of home in which Ozzy now resides.

Ozzy's mother did her research. Her decision must have been deliberate, trusting that with my brother's family, Ozzy could have a life she couldn't provide for some unfortunate reason.

We sometimes read of animals traveling long distances to return to their owners. Perhaps, from a mother's love, Ozzy's mother may travel from Western Pennsylvania to Maryland to find and see her son again. If she does, I hope Ozzy's mother comes around at night and sits on the window ledges of my brother's home, peering in to see little Ozzy enjoying himself, growing into the fine young cat she dreams him to be, filled with love of family, the love of my brother's home.

Perhaps, too, each night, my brother's son, Zack, will take a green ceramic bowl of leftovers that Becky prepared and place it next to their back-porch door for a stray cat that suddenly appeared one day and now is found sitting there each night.

Legacy

Gary was my first friend who passed early in life. We were in graduate school together. With his last name starting with an *M*, we were destined in each class to sit near each other, given my last name starts with an *O*. A friendship developed, a result of the alphabetical seating, as often does in schools where students are seated in alphabetical order. Perhaps these can be called alphabetical friendships.

Gary died when the car in which he was the front-seat passenger was hit head-on by a drunk driver. He died instantly. Another friend of mine, the driver, was in the hospital for several weeks. I went to see him there. Unnecessary suffering. I felt his pain to some degree as I tried to keep my conversation light and jovial. That's what we do in those situations: try to be normal. But there was no normalcy in this situation. My hospitalized friend was both severely injured and more traumatized over Gary's loss than I could have ever been.

I drove with other friends to Gary's funeral in Scranton, Pennsylvania. It was a strange town on a strange, partially sunny day for a very surreal and somber event. I knew no one except my few friends. I offered sympathies to Gary's parents and siblings, strangers to me; their grief I could only begin to imagine. Or believe. I realized that their dreams of a future with Gary and all he could bring to their lives had ceased, and their efforts in raising and nurturing Gary had ended. All in an instant. The result of someone needlessly taking one drink too many and then believing they could understand how to apply pressure to a gas pedal and maneuver a 4,100-pound vehicle with precision on a road darkened by the night.

I felt a real finality, a void, at that moment in the dimly lit viewing parlor filled with baskets of mourning flowers intended to support the moment, but only adding to the loss, it seemed.

For me, my exchanges on a daily basis and at an occasional party with Gary had ended. Near me in my classes, there was now an empty seat filled with memories. His spirit seemed to live there for me, and I suspect for all those around him whom he had befriended. Even the following year, when his seat was filled as the alphabetical list contracted with his absence, he was still there for me. For us.

Mom and Dad started taking my brother and me to funeral homes and funerals early in our lives. I don't remember the first. I remember, in one of those moments as a kid when I wasn't supposed to be listening, hearing Dad explain to his youngest sister that he wanted his boys to be comfortable with funeral homes and funerals, but without stating the obvious—death. He said it is all part of life, and he needed to allow it to be so for my brother and me. He succeeded. There was no one moment when funeral homes and their intended purpose were a shock to either my brother or me. Like the sun and the trees and so much of life to a kid, they just were.

I started thinking about all of this when my college buddy Joe, who lived next door to me in our dormitory known as Gerry (Gerard Hall), emailed me about an upcoming milestone anniversary of our graduation from Saint Vincent College. Joe started messaging me about a year prior, asking if I could help with the reunion planning. I was hesitant. First, I didn't have time. Second, the travel for my work was always at the top of my mind when planning anything in my life.

Joe was understanding but persistent in a friendly way. I had a few nostalgic tugs at my heartstrings to help, given the request was from Joe and given I have often stated that my years at Saint Vincent College were some of the best years of my life. But reality was reality, and I didn't have the time. As we neared the date of the event, Joe sent a message asking if I was going to attend. I had to decline, as I was scheduled to be out of the country on business that week.

But I did follow up with Joe afterward, inquiring as to the success of the event. And a success it was. Held on campus, a campus that has evolved and grown significantly since our feet last touched its much-trodden paths, Joe commented that the food was great, which it always was, the football game was exciting, the campus was still verdantly beautiful, and the weather held. I was happy for him and for all his planning.

This all came with a footnote. Prior to the event, my college sent a listing to our reunion classmates of those who had passed. Joe mentioned to me early in his messaging that a significant percentage of our class had passed. I couldn't believe it. We were too young. But the memorial letter I received from Saint Vincent confirmed this. I read it several times. I read the list of names. Yes. I still didn't believe it. I didn't know all of the guys listed, but I knew enough and remembered their majors. Kids then, we passed each other on the much-trodden paths between buildings for four years, spent time talking in our dorms, between classes and over breakfasts, during lunches and dinners in the dining hall, the food all homemade by the wonderful Sisters of Charity in residence.

And many of these same guys were packed into rooms on Saturday nights for parties, sometimes "keggers" as they were known for obvious reasons. All faces, for me, that are logged in my memory, faces of guys who never aged since last seeing them on campus, whose lives, like mine, moved on. I appreciate that I only could recall their young faces as I read the list of thirty-six names, about 10 percent of my graduating class. I couldn't help but wonder how many may have been victims of the recent pandemic. Eric and Ted were medical doctors. I remember both of them well, sharing classes with them.

I will put the list into my Bible someday. For now, it sits on my desk at home as a reminder of the guys listed and a wonderful time in life once lived for them and for me.

My graduating class established a scholarship in their memory. As more of us pass to the next life, our names will be added, leaving only the remaining class members to continue contributing to the scholarship. I trust that my class president, formerly a managing director with a Wall Street firm, will ensure that the fund will continue into perpetuity once the last of us is no longer around to make a contribution to it.

***

Among the fading photographs, articles, and letters now in my dad's scrapbook and in family photo albums are posted three articles, one from the *Paris Herald Tribune*, dated Friday, January 19, 1945, and two yellowed with age, one of which is undated. Both are accompanied by a letter to my dad's mother, my grandmother. Dad was a staff sergeant in the Army Medical Corps stationed in France during World War II. I remember him saying that Grandma had not heard from him in a while and, like all military mothers then and now, was very concerned. The letter was from Dad's army buddy, Robert E. Mowry, informing Grandma that her son, my soon-to-be dad, was okay. The *Paris Herald Tribune* article was about Dad and Mr. Mowry. The other two articles were about Mr. Mowry himself.

Mr. Mowry was a corporal in the army; he served with my dad in the medical corps in France. Nestled among my dad's army photos are pictures of Dad and his friend, whom I will now refer to as Corporal Robert Mowry, together with some of the other members of their company. Some of the photos were taken in unknown villages in the beautiful French countryside, places that were still untouched by the war, the locations of which remain locked in the photos.

Corporal Mowry's letter to Grandma was typewritten on a manual typewriter. Dated August 9, 1945, it read:

We had an uneventful seventeen day crossing, three submarine scares but no action until we got to Le Harve, [sic] France when a ship to our left struck a mine. We debarked about twelve the night of the sixteenth, marched two miles to a train station and boarded the "40 and 8" boxcars for our trip to Camp Lucky Strike, an assembly area. We spent the night in those cars and all I recall is that I had never been so close to freezing solid in my life. The trip was to take four hours but due to some complication we were on the train about nine hours. At 11 AM on the 17th, as we were coming into St. Valery-en-caux, France, the brakes failed at the top of a hill and we went sailing into the station down in the valley. None of us knew anything was wrong until just before the accident when we felt the train leave the tracks, then a terrific crash and it was all over. I understand Bill was standing in the doorway and was thrown clear, coming out with a sprained ankle. I was sitting back in the corner having a light lunch of K rations and my leg was broken just above the knee. There were eighty-five men in our company. Thirty three [sic] were killed and a similar number seriously injured. The car with

*Bill and myself went into the second story of
the station, quite a feeling to wind up with a
broken leg in somebody's bathroom. Bill and
I both lost many close friends, but the way
the accident happened nobody had a chance.
We just considered there were two groups that
day, the lucky and the unlucky. We consider
ourselves fortunate that we were in the latter.*

Corporal Lowry was twenty years old at the time, the
son of a Saint Louis, Missouri, minister. Dad was twenty-
two years old. The *Paris Herald Tribune* article reported this
same accident in more detail. One of the two yellowed-
with-age articles, dated September 15, 1945, was from
an unknown Saint Louis newspaper. It reported Corporal
Lowry's passing. While recovering from his broken leg after
being transported to a Chicago hospital, he chose to give
blood for the Red Cross war effort. At the very young age
of twenty, my dad's friend Corporal Robert Eugene Mowry
experienced a fatal heart attack during this simple and routine procedure. The letter he composed to Grandma was
sent five weeks before his passing.

My dad was an extremely generous man with his time
and talents. It is easy to see why he and Corporal Mowry
became friends. Only my imagination can begin to com-
prehend what Dad and Corporal Mowry were trained to
experience together in the countryside and battlefields of
France while serving in the medical corps during World
War II—a time in life that drew Dad and Corporal Robert
Mowry together, along with others in his company, as
friends, thirty-three of whom were lost in the accident.

Soon after the crash, Dad and those who were still alive and uninjured proceeded into battle.

Dad never talked about his time in WWII; therefore, neither this event nor his friend Robert were ever mentioned. The letter and articles were kept by Grandma, secured among the contents in her bedroom, within a special drawer of significant memories that touched her heart and soul. Some of Grandma's memories, in physical form, were inherited by Dad after Grandma's passing. The letter and articles were both sobering to read for the first time... well, actually, every time.

My brother and I have often speculated on the origins of my brother's name. I inherited William as my first name, proudly and intentionally handed down from my dad and his dad. I was the first, as my dad was, to carry the Olson name in our respective Olson generations, and with it came the honor and duty of receiving the first name of William.

My brother and I never thought to probe our parents about the origins of my brother's name. We only now realize that perhaps it was not chance that resulted in my brother being named Robert Eugene. We believe it was and continues to be a tribute to Dad's friend—Corporal Robert Eugene Mowry.

***

Reading of and remembering the faces of my departed Saint Vincent College classmates from a time when we were all young, and learning and growing into adulthood, brought home the reality that we are all just passing through this life on our way to another, that our time on this earth is limited and, we realize with the wisdom of years, fleeting. It brought back memories of Gary.

Unfortunately, but maybe fortunately, this is a lesson we learn late in life.

If used positively, our lives become our legacy for future generations. The nuns in the convent school of the little town of Berceto, Italy, where Grandma Bernini was educated, taught Grandma her cooking skills and how to embroider and set a proper table. I don't think either Grandma Bernini or the nuns ever thought that, three and four generations later, those same recipes unique to their Italian locale would cross the Atlantic Ocean and still be made with the same care and love with which Grandma was taught to make them, only now in places named Pennsylvania, Oklahoma, New Jersey, Texas, and Ohio.

And yet, they are. There is not a Bernini table, now into the third and fourth generations, that is not properly set for holiday dinners, sometimes still with Grandma's embroidered table linens.

And Grandma Olson's father, my great-granddad John Gill, had his obituary printed on the front page of the 1927 edition of the local newspaper, the *Indiana Evening Gazette*. A very religious man, he fathered a namesake son who became a minister. His notoriety, though, which resulted in his obituary being featured on the front page of the local newspaper, was due to being a poet, with much of his verse centered on religious themes.

Three generations later, his great grandsons Bob and Eric both served as missionaries, with Eric going on to become a minister. Both Bob and Eric took the messages that appeared in Great-Granddad Gill's incredible poetry beyond his home in Strangford, Pennsylvania, beyond the borders of the United States, and into the world. I am sure, as he sat composing his beautiful paragraphs in longhand, the thought that the meanings behind his poetry would be carried forward into the world through his future great-grandsons was never a flicker in his mind.

And yet, they were.

***

Our lives do carry forward. We all have a purpose. We all leave a legacy. I don't think any of us can fully imagine how what we do in our lives will impact others in the future. But it will. And hopefully in a positive way, whether it be a table setting or a recipe, a poem or a belief handed down, an exchange of friendship in college or in the armed services, or the memory of sitting next to another in graduate school.

Or in a name bestowed with reverence on a new life...

...Robert Eugene

Goodbye. Good night. Come back.
I'll see you tomorrow!

References, Sources, Bibliography

No Less than an A on That Report Card

Antenucci, Eugene. *Secrets of Italian Self Care*. 2023.

Antenucci, Eugene. *Finding the Good Life*. 2020.

Tchaikovsky, Pyotr Ilyich. *1812 Overture*. 1880.

Saint Valery-en-Caux

Eustice, Russell C. "Russell C. Eustice Recalls the Troop Train 2980 Tragedy at St. Valery-en-Caux during World War II." *HistoryNet Staff*. June 12, 2006.

Disco

The Trammps. "Disco Inferno." *Disco Inferno*. Atlantic, 1976.

Perfection

Vieira, Mark A. *Irving Thalberg: Boy Wonder to Producer Prince.*

University of California Press, 1950.

Grandma Olson

Warner, Anna Bartlett. Lyrics of "Jesus Loves Me." 1859.

Bradbury, William Batchelder. Tune of "Jesus Loves Me." 1862.

Angels and Children

Wikipedia. "Larimar." https://en.m.wikipedia.org. Retrieved July 15, 2024.

Grandma Olson II

Phillips, Irna, and Emmons Carlson, creators. *Guiding Light.* NBC/CBS Radio, 1937–1956. CBS Television, 1952–2009.

The Beautiful Paper-Flower Lady

Stevenson, Robert. *Mary Poppins.* Walt Disney Productions, 1964.

Sunflowers on First Avenue

Wikipedia. "Waterside Generating Station." http://en.m.wikipedia.org. Retrieved July 15, 2024.

Jackson, Joe. "Steppin' Out." *Night and Day*. A&M, 1982.

Steam Pipes and Peter Pan

Buck, Chris, and Jennifer Lee. *Frozen*. Walt Disney Animation Studios, 2013.

Mrs. Byron

"Wilma B. Byron." *Indiana Gazette*. December 7, 2021.

Drake, Milton, Al Hoffman, and Jerry Livingston. "Mairzy Doats." Miller Music Publishing, 1943.

Loesser, Frank. "A Bushel and a Peck." *Guys and Dolls*. Musical score, 1950.

Munk, Arnold (a.k.a. Watty Piper). *The Little Engine that Could*. 1930.

D'Urfey, Thomas. "Old MacDonald Had a Farm." 1706.

"Frere Jacques." Traditional French song.

Lyte, Eliphalet Oram. "Row, Row, Row Your Boat." 1852.

"Yankee Doodle." Traditional United States song. 1780s.

Cottrau, Teodoro, translator. "Santa Lucia." Traditional Neopolitan song. 1849.

Child, Lydia Maria. "Over the River and Through the Woods" (a.k.a. "The New England Boy's Song about Thanksgiving"). *Flowers for Children,* vol. 2. 1844.

Henning, Paul, and Ruth Henning. *Petticoat Junction.* CBS Television, 1963–1970.

White Christmases

Jackson-Miller, Jill, and Sy Miller. "Let There Be Peace on Earth." 1955.

Pierpoint, Folliott S. "For the Beauty of the Earth." 1864.

Child, Lydia Maria. "Over the River and Through the Woods" (a.k.a. "The New England Boy's Song about Thanksgiving"). *Flowers for Children,* vol. 2. 1844.

Coots, J. Fred, and Haven Gillespie. "Santa Claus Is Coming to Town." 1934.

Midnight Mass

Peale, Norman Vincent. *A Practical Guide to Mastering the Problems of Everyday Living.* Prentice Hall, 1952.

Handel, George Frederic. *Messiah.* 1742.

Watts, Isaac. "Joy to the World." 1719.

Gruber, Franz Xaver. "Silent Night" (a.k.a. "Stille Nacht, Heilige Nacht"). 1818.

Progress

Capra, Frank. *It's a Wonderful Life.* (Based on "The Greatest Gift" by Phillip Van Doren Stern). Liberty Films, 1946.

"Then and Now, 1807–1957." *Black Lick Sesquicentennial.* 1957.

Archangels

Jenkins, Dallas, creator and cowriter. *The Chosen.* Angel Studios, 2017.

Ozzy on the Doorstep

Jones, Chuck. *Marvin the Martian.* Looney Tunes, 1948.

Legacy

Herald Tribune.

www.ingramcontent.com/pod-product-compliance
Lightning Source LLC
Chambersburg PA
CBHW060305100426
42742CB00011B/1874

* 9 7 8 1 6 3 7 6 5 7 4 7 8 *